Llyvyr Taliesin.

———◆———

Vol. ix^B of the
Series of Old Welsh Texts.

Nos. 1—80 on O.W. hand-made paper;
Nos. 81—330 on deckled-edge paper;
Four copies on vellum; and a
number on thin paper.

Poems

from the

Book of Taliesin

Edited,
amended, & translated by

J. Gwenogvryn Evans

Hon. D. Litt. (Wales).

Criticism does not mention the salvages.
TALIESIN, 30˙12.

Tremvan, Llanbedrog, N. Wales
1915

THERE ARE QUALITIES THAT MAKE things live; that which lives becomes classical; and what has become classical is mostly remote needing hard linguistic and grammatical study, which is apt to dry up the little spring of poetry. By translating the words into dictionary language the original is emptied of most of its meaning; we miss form, light, and shade; because we have not the knowledge or the sympathy, we fail to catch, across the gulf of years, the peculiar thrill of what was once a 'winged word' flying from soul to soul. It is perhaps in this department that the most pressing work of pure scholarship remains to be done.[1]

EVERYTHING, INCLUDING THIS LITTLE BOOK, has a history. In the far-away 'seventies' I bought a copy of the Four Ancient Books of Wales.[2] After 'looking' at the Welsh text with blank amazement I placed the two volumes reverently on my shelves. My admiration for their editor knew no bounds, for did he not understand and translate the whole? I read the prolegomena with unquestioning faith, and felt humiliated that it had been left to a Scot to render such service to Welsh studies. A few years later I read the proof-sheets of Celtic Britain, which followed the Scot's lead, and thus raised him still higher in my estimation. I now turned to the translations

[1] See The Rise of the Greek Epic by Prof. Gilbert Murray, pp. 5-7.

[2] Edited by William F. Skene, Edinburgh, 1868.

v

of the Four Ancient Books with results entirely disastrous to my patriotism. I fell into the common error of judging the originals by the translations. The habit of believing the story of the first narrator is engrained in human nature. 'Where there is smoke there is fire,' sums up the collective experience of mankind. Few stay to observe closely, so as to distinguish between smoke and mirage, or mist. I was no exception. I turned my back on the Kymric Muse—I sought fresh woods and pastures new; I tended sheep with Michael in the dells of Cumberland; 1 wandered on the banks of bonie Doon; I talked of the Alps and Apennines, the Pyrenean and the river Po; I felt the impulse of the wild West Wind; I learnt The letters that Cadmus gave—Think ye he meant them for a slave?

I went to Peniarth and saw the Book of Taliesin—I borrowed the MS., and copied it. To my surprise I found the meaning of a multitude of passages was clear as day-light and, like Tartini's sixth Sonata, their pure, simple harmonies haunted me. To account for the obscurity of the other parts, I conceived the theory that the 'sixth century' work of Taliesin had been vamped in the twelfth, for I was nurtured in sixth century traditions. I elaborated my theory on 609 folios of foolscap. When the last page was written, I looked with pride upon my pile of sheets. After a week or two I set to the work of testing my thesis at every point, and by degrees demolished my own superstructure to the last line. To my credit be it recorded the 609 folios of foolscap, with all their prettily turned passages, were consigned to the flames, leaving me sadder, but no whit wiser.

About this time the late Professor Zimmer spent a day at Tremvan. I plied him with many a question about Taliesin, but received uniformly for answer: *nis gwnn—nis gallav ðweyd*, I do not know—I cannot say. I next turned to a Welsh scholar of repute, and proposed that we should jointly attempt to amend and translate the text of Taliesin. He advised me to attempt no such thing—he, certainly, would not coöperate; 'in short I funk it' were his parting words. The distraction of reporting on Welsh MSS. thrust Taliesin aside for a time. But one day I was with my Gamaliel, and as the skies were serene I sought for guidance and light, and lo! the atmosphere became electric. He seized volume ii. of the Four Ancient Books and read: *agwr bwrr bythic . . am ys gwin ffeleic, am ys gwin mynic gyltwn*, 59·19. Eyeing me intently he asked: What do you make of that? or of these 'bones of the mist,' *escyrn nywl?* (22·15). Then turning over energetically some more leaves he remarked: The only sensible thing I can see in Taliesin is this—*pren onhyt yw vy awen*, 62·25, my muse is—is—wooden! Flinging the book to an adjoining table I was asked with crushing emphasis: Do you think that *you* are going to get at the bottom of stuff like that?3 Men and brethren! I thus became a Pharisee, the son of a Pharisee of the straitest sect, and renounced Taliesin, as I thought and believed, for ever. But the virus was in my blood. The unprisoned spirit of Taliesin haunted me. I knew his muse was not 'wooden.'

3 When first I asked to see a MS. it was remarked: "What is the good? You can't read it." The tone in which that was said became the driving force that shaped the after-activities of my life.

While sitting around the yule log one evening I unburdened my soul to the late Professor Strachan.

My friend became alert, interested, sympathetic, protesting that "after so much labour it is wrong to throw your work away. You have learnt more than you think. The difficulties are, as is well known, very great, and *you will have to run the risk of making howlers; but in Keltic he, who is not prepared to face that risk, will accomplish very little.* As for criticism, why should you mind that? The few who know anything about Taliesin will appreciate your contribution—what the rest may think or say—it does not really matter."

The pages of Taliesin were scanned once more. Many plans were formed, considered, and rejected.

At last the policy of the 'clean slate' was adopted. I resolved to have no plan, no theory, no object but one—to get at the *meaning* of the text, and follow the evidence whithersoever it might lead. A beginning was made with the poems that seemed easiest. Metre and orthography were regularised, and such portions as I understood translated, the remainder being left blank for future effort. This *tour de force* lasted over a year, and seven times was it repeated. Gradually one by one certain historical and topographical landmarks emerged clearly above the mists, but in isolation. I turned to the elegies to Owein Gwyneδ by Gwalchmei and Kynδel with suggestive results. I, therefore, read carefully the works of Meilir, Gwalchmei, Kynδel, Hywel ap O. G., and the Bard of Mochnant, compiling an Index verborum to each poet as I went along. A comparison of these vocabularies with one another, as well as with that of Taliesin shewed that Meilir, Gwalchmei and

Taliesin belonged to the same period. Much of their topography is also in common. This led to my spending three summer outings in traversing the counties of Flint and Denbigh, as well as the English borders from Montgomery to Oswestry—from Whitchurch to Chester. I climbed the hills and surveyed the land from the promontory castle of Beeston, from Breiðin, from many points on Berwyn, from y Rhodwyð and Buðugre, from Treiðin, Caer Gwrlè, Caer Estyn, and Montalt; and from Moel y Gaer to Coppa ILwyvenyð. With the help of a bicycle I covered close on a thousand miles.[4] It was only after these interesting, but strenuous wanderings that I really began to understand our text, and learnt to appreciate the felicity of many a descriptive passage. How seldom do we realize that so much depends on what *we bring* to the understanding of a subject. Just as mathematical formulæ convey nothing to a non-mathematical mind, so the student who finds no meaning in Taliesin doth but proclaim his own ignorance of Brythonic twelfth-century thought and action. Acquaintance with the records and literatures of the Norman period is an illuminating factor in providing an insight into our text. It is necessary not only to master facts, but also to imbibe the spirit of the time. Paleography, Philology, Grammar can do much for us, but it is the comparative study of contemporary literatures and of history that will help most to the understanding of our author. After all it is Taliesin's poetry & message, not his words, that have the human interest.

Survey-
ing the
ground

4 Part was done a-foot in the company of Mr. Llywarch Reynolds. On our way from Gwerni Dygen to Breiddin the bull of Crugion disputed our progress and passage of the Severn at the Ferry. On gaining the right bank the Lord

After such a fashion did this bantling originate. But there was no idea of publishing till it became evident that the Notes, consisting of emendations, alternative suggestions, illustrative passages from the poets and historical evidence, would fill upwards of 700 pages. The expense this would involve led to the embodiment of the emendations in an edited text, thus presenting the thoughts of every poem continuously, in place of in a series of disjointed comments. To point out irregularities would be supererogatory. Metre, assonance, and rhyme act as so many detectives of the scribe's infidelities, as well as of his omissions and interpolations. Those able to count up to ten can test the metres; and the reading aloud of the MS. text makes us aware of 'things gone wrong.' The Tables of Scribal Errors shew how things do go wrong—how words get transmogrified in transcription, and why we should choose one word rather than another, though of the same meaning.

Paleographical mistakes[5] are mainly due to certain resemblances of different letters in combination, and can be reduced to a fairly fixed rule. Emendations worked out on these lines will be outside the experience and ken of many of my critics, but are none the less valid for that— 'They don't know everything down in Judee.'

put it in my heart to run, for my friend carried his seventy years with an agility that made light of ditches and seven-barred gates, thus reducing the enemy to impotent rage. The memory of the after-thirst on the slopes of Breiddin remains, as well as of the downpour we experienced west of Corwen, while ascending the Berwyn. It is no wonder that the RAIN on this mountain-range caused Henry ii. to flee.

[5] Mistakes due to metathesis are familiar. So are repetitions and anticipations of neighbouring syllables. The tendency to telescope words, like 'whey' for 'when they,' is the mark of age—the hand is too slow for the brain.

Where there is a lacuna, consisting of a line (part or whole), or the end of one line and the beginning of the next, we must needs have recourse to divination, relying on context, rhythm, and rhyme. Insertions of this kind, which have no sanction in the original are printed in *italics*[6], being offered tentatively as suggestions. Then there are numerous cases where there is something wrong, but exactly what is wrong, it is hard to say. In these cases there is an equal danger in the avoidance of all change as in changing too much. It is likely enough that I have erred both ways—that I have stuck in the mud here, and meddled there unadvisedly. Most *workers* do such things,[7] because it is only '*Sometimes* a light surprises a Christian while he' toils. Owing to the fitfulness of this discerning light Taliesin provides pitfalls enough to ruin the reputation of a dozen Academicians. As a guiding principle the fewer the changes the better, provided that we get good sense, which is ever characteristic of Taliesin's muse.

Paleo-
graphy

In orthography I have not followed my own whims, but rather the practice of the best MSS. before Welsh lost its way in Tudor times. All the modern patents are unhistorical; they are also

Ortho-
graphy

6 It was intended to italicise also all changes not made on paleographical lines; but here and there I was too intent on the meaning of the text to remember my own rule. For example, if cledyf were changed into clefyd, celfyd, crefyd, or dedyf nothing should be italicised, because the five words are, paleographically speaking, liable to be confused by our scribe. But if, for any reason, gwaew displaces cledyf, gwaew should be in italics, because no confusion of form is possible between the two words.

7 The man who never makes a mistake is a prattling dummy. J. Stuart Mill spent his life "struggling on, making mistakes and correcting them." And Sir Edward Grey has told us that 'If we get into a mess everybody knows about it, but it is only we ourselves know the mess into which we did not get.' 17. ii. 12.

unscientific, because they ignore the dominating influence of the accent. To intrude etymology into spelling is sheer pedantry. Our spelling once represented sound in the simplest possible way.[8] To double consonants except under the accent is to defy the practice of the golden age of Welsh literature, and of every Welsh mouth[9]. What a reader wants are ideas, not an uncouth agglomeration of redundant consonants. The man who writes y*ng-Ng*hymry is like a drunkard who sees double, but then he is drunk.

Mutations take place in the Genitive case, in the Accusative, in words expressing duration of time, and with verbs of motion, as 'aeth Von.' Words in opposition are also mutated, and even verbs, though the relative be dropped, as 'Taliesin *g*an,' yscriven Brydein *b*ryder, etc.

Trans-
lation

The translation was begun solely for my own discipline and correction. Seeking for the inward thought and spirit of the poems, I tried to interpret them to myself, so as to render sense for sense, rather than follow the letter which killeth. In the revisions I strove further to provide not a crib for the class-room, but a version for the lover of literature who needs, along with the sense, something of the bloom of the poet's inspiration, so hard 'to keep unhurt in another tongue.' If I have failed, I have done my best, and I feel no shame to fall where 'other footsteps dare not.'

8 The older the MS. the simpler the spelling. See B.B.C., note 2·2. cp. 'YngHaerwys, YngWynedd.' Gr. Hiraethog.

9 Cp. ynghyngor 1·28, yng hyoeð 33·2, yng Wensteri 30·12, yng Wyneð 64·20, yngwarth 17·17, yng wlat 44·25, 76·8, ymro 30·6, ymryn 22·25, ymyt 36·6, y Mon 45·18, 73·15, ymrythwch 11·6, 48·20, ymhwyllat 92·7, vyng byfalle 3·20, vyng hynnyð 74·10, anghyfieith 79·3, amhâr 16·6, &c., &c.

The question is not so much how many mistakes have been made as how many have been avoided—how many errors have been corrected—how many obscurities have been removed.[10]

Taliesin is a well-authenticated historical character. He tells us that he 'was not born in adversity,' 27·3, though he grew up in abject poverty. At 71·9 he says that he was 'a prince in disguise'; and yet he had no settled home, but simply 'slept at Pulford.' His play-ground was the watery lane that led thence to the city of the Legion.[11] He was a subject of the earl of Chester till the battle of Godeu, whence he was carried off to Powys, and made a herdsman there. After a time he escaped into the Forest of Ḻwyvenyð, and became subject and bard to Owein Gwyneð. There are two additional passages, 42·6·7—the one speaks of him as 'a preceptor in Dygen,' i.e. at

10 Even if it be proved that I have made a mistake in every line the TIME of COMPOSITION, the CHIEF ACTORS, and the GEOGRAPHY will remain unaffected. A critic may dispute my rendering, but it does not follow that he is right because he differs from me, or cannot in 7 minutes see what it has taken me 7 years to 'grip.' However the really obscure passages are but a fraction of the whole.

11 Note .1. that Caer Lleon is not used for Chester by Taliesin (see nn. 69·12,b; 73·11); 2. that Caer Lleon is unknown to Aneirin; 3. that the one instance of its occurrence in the B·B·C· is later than 1200, and that it sets the metre wrong. The list of cities in the Nennian ADDITAMENTA has Cair Ligualid, Cair legion, & Cair legeion guar ufic. In Taliesin and the Bard of Mochnant Caer Liwelydd means Chester. Can it be that the Cair legion of the list means Holt, to which the name of 'Caer lleon' has adhered? The 'Gweith Cair Legion' of Annales Cambrie, Ao. 613, may have taken place at or near Holt, or between Holt and Bangor Iscoed, whose monks were present in their hundreds. (Bede Bk· ii. cap. ii·) Had the battle been at Chester the monks would hardly have turned out in a body : observe also that the Welsh leader was the prince of Powys, and that Powys never reached beyond Pulford· The best ford on the lower Dee is at Holt, near which the XXth Legion had its tile kilns.

Strata Marcella; the other as 'a hoary wanderer' at Norham on the Tweed in 1209. In as much as the house of Powys was anathema to the bard, it is, on the face of it, incredible that he would enter a Powysian foundation; and chronology condemns the reference to the northern expedition as a later accretion ' in the manner of Taliesin.'

On the other hand 'patriots' of the mythological school tell us that Taliesin flourished in the sixth century. In the Introduction to volume i., the evidence has been reviewed briefly, but with care. 'It will be wise to hearken not to me but to my arguments.' However, we have Mr. Lloyd George's assurance that 'there is nothing a man likes less than to be convinced by argument.' And I have myself observed that there is always in fact something trivial not to the taste of poetic minds. It has ever been so. The Greek Atomists[12] were proof against the discovery that the earth was round—they preferred a world shaped "like a tambourine" that rested elegantly 'on air.' Similarly the Welsh Atomist[13] hugs tradition, repels discovery, and loves not the truth.[14]

The Welsh Atom

> From idle dreams, and rant—
> From tambourines aslant,
> Good Lord! deliver us.

[12] Leukippos, the father of the atom, deliberately rejected the Pythagorean discovery that the earth was spherical, and taught that it was in shape "like a tambourine," resting on the air, and sloping towards the south. J. Burnet.

[13] The Welsh 'atom' is true to type—it has 'no weight,' though characterised by 'excess of magnitude.' Its votary cannot construe a dozen lines of early Welsh poetry, nor write a modern dozen with decency, but he struts before the public with hat a-tilt, deceiving himself and some others by the tinkle of his tambourine.

[14] "It is difficult to get the truth believed. It is quite easy to get something which is not the truth believed." Sir Edward Grey.

The proof-sheets of a portion of this booklet were seen by Mr. T. Gwynn Jones, and received a good deal of frank, honest comment. But as there is no way of indicating minute criticism except by reproducing it, I can only refer to it in general terms, while tendering my cordial thanks. For what Mr. Gwynn Jones is directly responsible see the Notes. It is also a pleasant duty to thank the Council and Librarian of the National Library of Wales, for allowing this little book, as well as the Notes and Index of Vol. i., to be machined in their printing department. Neither must I pass over in silence the efficient and rare service of my some-time assistant, Mr. George Jones; nor omit to mention the information I received, on certain points of medieval theology, from my friend and neighbour, Mr. Ernest Edwin Williams of the Inner Temple.

J. Gwenogvryn Evans.

Tremvan, Llanbedrog.
May 25, 1915.

TABLE OF CONTENTS

CORRECTIONS.

——o——

⁎ Certain inconsistencies in the orthography were mainly introduced by the Compositors, who could not unlearn old ways. My punctuation was also persistently edited. As it was not feasible to revise the final 'corrections' on the machine many errors have remained, and a few fresh ones have crept in.

The following references specify passages that have been amended in the *Miscellaneous Notes*, (pp. 82–145 of Vol. i.)

15·79, 26·3, 28·28·70·76, 30·68, 34·121, 36·180, 38·186·195, 40·230, 50·43, 52·96, 54·108·119·131, 55·108, 56·13, 58·36, 62·19, 64·10, 70·113, 72·20, 78·3, 82·49, 84·22·29·32·33, 86·14, 88·47, 90·20, 94·13·50, 108·41, 114·28, 116·46, 118·43, 120·59, 120·4–7, 122·29·32·35, 124·6, 126·17, 128·56, 134·32, 140·15, 142·6, 144·18·26·8, 146·19·25–40, 158·29, 168·148, 176·39, 180·93, 188·6.

Alternative readings have been offered in other [places. *xii.*, l.15 for 'opposition' read 'apposition.'

1·22 for '1220' read '1230.'

1·25 Delete 'Owein Kyveilog.'

7·15 for *singers* read *joglars.*

12·24 for 'Wenδyδ' read 'Gwenδyδ.'

16·14 for *suδen* ? read *suδem*, we must sink.

29·49 for *princes* read *prince.*

30·70 for *Gwern* read *Derw*, oak.

31·76 for *medlar* read *briar.*

41·27 read : *I was not born in adversity.*

42·3 for '*i* ħanghen' read *anghen.*
          who sustained poverty, etc.

42·19 for 'govarυan' read *govaran.*

50·61 for *a dwvn* ? read *aδwyn*.

53·96 read : 'in the treasury of *lyric* song.'

55·119 From *Holy*-head to 'Lache eyes.'

60·10 *? read* : Dedwyδ Đovyδ . . . *the Blessed Lord, too, created my own son, Avagδu.*

64·1 for *gelvyδ* read *celvyδ*.

64·31 for 'en·*r*eineu' read *eneineu*.

66·52 for *an* read *ânt*.

69·64 read : *The Saxons, having been crippled at Seon, show signs of exhaustion.*

71·113 for 'bears an' ? read *introduces his*

76·12 for *a'i* read *no'i*.

78·41 for 'eisyⅡyδ' read 'eisyllyδ.'

78·3 *History suggests reading:* ɡor·vodes o·ɡyv·nes Welyδon, *(Rhun) mastered the rather near neighbourhood of the Laches.*

85·19 for *flows* read *flowed*.

86·10 for 'Clydwyn' ? read *cyrchyn.*
These could not sustain the counter-action of the power of the ally they 'went for.'

101·36 for *or* read *nor.*

158·7 for *δyd* read *dyδ.*

182 (title) read *'Am δy·δyvi.'*

189 for '*a* an' read *an.*

Change d to δ and read: ɡorvloeδ 6·72, δy·enn iⅡin 10·8, δelideu 12·21, δy·ɡwyn 20·159, δy·livas 20·175, Đeganhwy 54·107, Đovyδ 60·10, vlwyδyn 68·87, δy·hawl 84·41, byδiv 90·28, δiɡones 102·8, see Preface, p. *xii.*

The words following should also be read in the mutated form : verwei 10·18, ɡŵyndawd 12·25, or·ffennas 20·176, ? waδawl 48·21, i *d*rachwres 86·14, y ar vur 128·31.   See corrections in vol. i. of 116·46, 118·34, 140·19.

Early Welsh had a 3 pl. future-present ending in -int, which appears occasionally as -ynt.

THE ARGUMENT

THE OPINIONS OF MOST MEN ARE WORTH HAVING, so it has been said, *"while their reasons seldom convince any but themselves."* Acting on this maxim, I submit, without comment, in the pages which follow, a transliterated, amended version of the BOOK OF TALIESIN, with a sense for sense translation. In doing so I am under no illusion. The obscurities of the original are notorious; and I, of all men, have most reason for knowing them, having spent years in going systematically through the text many times. The result offered, though not unconsidered, is necessarily tentative. The stumblings may be frequent, yet the number of problems solved, with a reasonable degree of certainty, is considerable. The question of the date of composition, which goes to the root of the whole matter, has been settled. So long as a student labours under the belief of a sixth century origin, so long will he walk in blinkers, and fail to perceive the plainest references to historical events between 1098 and 1220. The bard, or bards, after the fashion of this time, sang of contemporaries under assumed names. Owen Gwyneð and his sons, Henry II, Owen Kyveilog, Richard I, Gwen Wynnwyn, and King John are among the chief actors who figure in the poems which follow.

J.G.E.

Canu y Gwynt.

DYCHYMIG pwy yw?   1
     crëad cyn dilyw—
36 Crëadur cadarn,
24   heb gig, heb ascwrn,   4
     heb wytheu, heb waed,
25   heb ben, a heb draed.
     Ni byδ hŷn, na ieu,   7
26   noget y dechreu.
     Ni δaw o·i oδeu
37   er ovn, nag angheu :   10
1   Ni δi·oes i eiseu
     gan grëadurieu.
2   Mawr Đuw morwynneu !   13
     ban δaw o δechreu ?
     Mawr i verthideu,
3   y Gwr a·i goreu.   16
     Y·mäes, yng·hoed,
     heb law, a heb droed :
4   Heb haint a heb hoed,   19
     ev eiδig aδoed.
5   Ac ev yn gyv·oed
     a phymhoes pymhoed :
6   Hevyd yssyδ hŷn   23
     ped pymhwnt vlwyδyn.
     Ac ev yn gyv·led
7   ac wyneb tydwed.
     Ac ev ni aned :   27
     Ac ev ni weled.
8   Ar vor, ac ar dir,
     ni wŷl, ni welir.   30

2

The Song of the Wind.

WHOSE idea was the wind? 1
Created before the deluge,
he is a powerful creature,
sans flesh, sans bone, 4
sans veins, sans blood,
sans head, and sans feet.
He grows nor older, nor
younger, than at the first. 8
Nor fear, nor death
will turn aside his purpose.
The world of the living will never
survive the need of him. 12
Great GOD of the whirlwinds!
whence comes his beginning?
Great the resources of Him 15
who made the Wind, (which
traverses) field and forest,
without hand, or foot.
Without sickness or sorrow, 19
he is impatient of delay.
And he is co-eval with the
five ages of the five periods.
Moreover, he is older, though 23
it be half a million years.
And he is as widespread
as the face of the earth.
Born he was not, 27
nor ever was seen.
On sea, and on land,
he neither sees, nor is seen. 30

37 Ev yn ang·hywir,   31
    ni ẟaw ban vynnir.
    Ar dir, ac ar vor,
10 ev yn an·hepcor.   34
    Ev yn ẟi·achor :
    Ev yn ẟi·eisor :
11 Ev, o bedeiror,
    ni byẟ wrth gynghor.   38
    Ev gychwyn a*m*gor,
12 oẟ·uch maen yn·yvnvor.
    Ev ỻavar, ev mud,
    ev yn an·vynud :   42
    Ev yn wrẟ, yn ẟrud,
    ban dremyn dros dud.
14 Ev mud, ev ỻavar,
    ev yn or·ẟëar—   46
    mwyhav i vaniar
    ar wyneb daear.
    Ev yn ẟa, yn ẟrwg,
    ev yn an·eglwg.   50
    Ev yn an·amlwg,
    can nis gwŷl golwg.
17 Yn ẟrwg ac yn ẟa,
    ev hwnt, ev yma.   54
    Ev yẟ an·rhevna—
    ni ẟïwg a wna :
    Ni ẟïwg a wrech,
    ac ev yn ẟi·bech.   58
19 Yn wlyb ac yn sych,
    ev a ẟaw·n vynych.
20 Gwres heul ac oervel
    a dry naws awel :   62
    Teithi symudir,
    ac ev ni ẟimyir.

4

He is unreliable —   31
  he will not come when desired.
On land and sea,
  he is indispensable.   34
He knows no restraint —
  his lot has not been cast.
He comes from the four quarters ;
  he will brook no counsel.   38
He starts on his round, from the
  crest of a rock in the deep.
He is loquacious, he is mute,
  he is frolicksome.   42
He is vehement, intrepid,
  when he scours the land.
He is mute, he is loquacious,
  he is uproarious —   46
The most tumultuous
  on the face of the earth.
He is good, he is evil,
  he is blind :   50
He is invisible—
  no eye can see him.
He is evil, he is good,
  he is there, he is here.   54
When he works confusion,
  he will not repair what he does.
He will not restore what he wrecks,
  and yet he is without sin.   58
Now wet, and now dry,
  he comes frequently.
The sun's heat, and cold
  affect the feel of the wind,   62
  which ever changes his part,
  but never is destroyed.

40·22 MENHYD tragywyð !　　65
 23　ys Tydi *wehyð*
　　ðyliv *oll yssyð;*
 21　*Pawb a·th* edm*y*g*y*nt—
　　Gwr a gadwyn wynt.　　69
41·12 *Er* maint *vo ym·chwyð*
　　tonneu y Weryð—
40·22 Er gor·vloed eryv
 22　ban ðel yn rh*uthr*yð,　　73
41·13 Cyn traeth, cyverchyð,
　　a·i yrva ðervyð.
 14　A·m cuðw*y* tywawd,
　　ac ev yn deithawg.　　77

卐　卐　卐

𝕭𝖚𝖆𝖗𝖙𝖍 𝕭𝖊𝖎𝖗𝖉𝖉.

EV y·m peiꞮꞮied ym·*hob* pwyꞮꞮad,　　1
　gan veirð Brython, *a·r cawceinad.*
 7 Pryðest over *yng·hyw·rysseð:*　　3
　A·m rhy·or·seiv a·m　rhy·or·seð.
 15 I·r govan　goval ðigawn gorð ;　　5
　Wyv eisig bren, cyv·yng ar gerð.
 16　Buarth beirð *ban vo,*
　　pwy ar nis gwypo ?　　8
 17　Pymtheg mil drostaw,
　　yn i gym·hwysaw.
 18 Wyv cerðoliad ; wyv saer *mal* dryw ;　11
　wyv ceiniad claer : wyv dru*d* ; wyv syw
 19 *mal* sarff, *mal* serch ; yð ym·ge*i*sav :
 20 Neu·d wyv varð *swyn* ; yð ar·veiðav.
　Ban gân ceinieid ganu yng·hôv,　　15
 21　nid ev wnant wy ryveð uchov.

6

ETERNAL MIND!   65
'Tis Thou that weavest
  the web of all there be :
All men honour Thee
  who dost chain the Wind.
However much *he upheaves*   70
   the Ocean billows,
or shrieks in his violence
  when he comes in gusts,
  ere he touches shore, Thou speakest!
  and his race is run.   75
May the sands cover me,
  an the wind be in full career.

Congress of the Bards.

I Was sifted in every faculty by the   1
  Brython bards, and the crowned minstrel.
Poetising is futile in competition ;
  my competitor, however, chairs me.   4
Care enough to the young smith is his hammer ;
  I, too, am but a slender twig, inexperienced in craft.

    The congress of the bards, when it takes place,
      who is there that knows not of it ?
    Fifteen thousand favouring it,   9
      and arranging for it.

I am a musician—an artificer like the wren ;
I am a brilliant singer ; I am formidable, subtle
  as a serpent, as love ; I will enter the lists :   13
I am an enchanted bard ; I will dare (them all).
When the singers sing a song from memory,
  they perform no great wonder beyond what I can do.

7

7 Handid i mi eu herbyniaw,
  yn ði·vyvyr, heb ðysc, heb braw,　　18
  mal arvolÏi diÏad heb law—
23 val soði yn Ïyn heb aÏu naw.
  Tyrvid aches ; ehovn i grað ;　　21
24 uchel y gwaeð ; mordwy deryð.
25 Craig am waneg, wrth vawr drevnad—
  ang·hlud yscrwth, escar noðiad :　　24
27 Craig *rhag* perchen pen an·ynad ;
8·3 nid ev garav amrysoniad.
7·27 Ys gwna meðud veðdawd meðyð ;　　27
  a gor·wyth með warthruð brydyð.

8 Ev ceÏ, ev druÏ ; ev darweir Ïed ;
  ev ÏogeÏ cerð ; ev Ïemynnied.　　30

2 Carav i or·wŷð, a chil gorr gled,
  a barð a brŷd—ni brŷn i ged.
4 A geibl gelvyð, meueð ni ved.　　33
  Madws myned, er ym·dravawd
  a chelvyðeid am gelvyðawd ;
6 a chanu clwm, cystwm cy·wlad,　　36
  i vugeil bro, porth neithoriad.
7 Mal ym·ðeith *tranc* heb drwyd i gad,
8 eiriv vynnei ymðeith heb oed—
  eiriv vagei gneuha heb goed—　　40
9 mal ceisaw bydav yng·rug,
  mal peireint an·rheith yn vud,
  mal goscorð Ïüyð heb benn,
11 mal porthi ang·hlyd ar cenn,　　44
  mal grynniaw tyndei a gwrach,
12 mal haeðu awyr a bach,
  mal eirach gwaed ac yscaÏ,
13 mal gwneuthur goleu i ðaÏ,　　48
  mal dogni diÏad i noeth,
  mal tannu ewyn ar draeth,

8

It falls to me to compete with them,   17
   extemporaneously, without training or experience,
like a man donning armour without a hand,
or sinking in water without being able to swim.   20
The flowing tide seethes ; eager its pace ;
   loudly it roars ; then rushes ashore.
By a great design, the rock beyond the surf,   23
an immovable pile, *is* an insular refuge :
it is a defence against every madman :
I do not love contention.   26
'Tis drinking makes drunk the brewer ; *and*
over-draining of mead disgraces the bard, who is
a cellar, a liquor store ; a lewd, paunchy fellow ;
a receptacle of song ; a mere vagabond.   30
I love the woods,—a retreat in a cosy border, and
a bard who creates—not one who cadges for gifts.
The man who curses the artist will never prosper.
It is well to go (to Congress) for the sake of   34
   deliberating with artists about art ; and
to sing a string of verses, as the custom is, to the
governor of the district, the provider of the feast.

   As Death doth travel without track to war,   38
so a number went without assignation,
and many nursed the idea of nutting without trees,
like men seeking for a swarm of bees in heather,
like engines of destruction mute,   42
like a company of soldiers without a leader,
like men feeding the comfortless with husk,
like ridging tumbled-down houses with a *gwrach,*
like men reaching for the sky with a hook,   46
like men stanching blood with thistles,
like men striking a light for the blind,
like men allotting a coat of mail to the unarmed,
like men scattering foam on the strand,   50

9

15 mal porthi pyscawd ar laeth,
    mal töi neuað a dail,   52
16 mal ſlað ſlurig a gwyeil,
    mal toði tavled rhag gair.
17 Wyv barð neuað, wyv gyw cadeir :
18 Dy·ðygnad beirð ; llavar llysceir.   56
    Cyn vy ar·gywein i·m garw gyv·log
    rhy·phrynwyv i·m log i·th dy, Vab Meir !

Ʇ Ʇ Ʇ

Ctwynbawy.

ꓭARÐ, y·man y bo,   1
    neirtheint a gaffo :
19 Caned ban dyrffo :
    Sywed yn yd vo :
    Haelon vanacco,   5
3 neu·s bi a rotho.
    Drwy ieith Daliessin,
4 beirð, dy·ennilſin.
    Ciawr, ban ðarvu
    llïaws i olychu.   10
5 Bid *eiðaw* wylſeith—
    anrheith Avagðu :
    Neu·s dug, yn gelvyð,
6 gyvreu ar gywyð.
    Gwiawn leveryð—   15
    o *ðamwei*n dyvyð.
8 *Gwiðon*, y peiran,
    berwei, heb *wall*tan ;
7 gwnäei o varw vyw,
    ac an·hy·weith yw.   20

10

like men feeding fish with milk,   51
like men thatching the hall with leaves,
like men battering armour with withies,
like men melting a tablet against speech.   54
I am the bard of the Hall ; I am the winner of the chair :
The bards are greatly incensed ; loud their anathemas.

Before my ferrying over to my hard wages,
may I secure a place in thy mansion, Son of Mary !   58

Ⴟ Ⴟ Ⴟ

The Festival.

THE Bard, wherever he may be,
   shall have entertainment.
Let him sing when the spirit moves :
Let him prophesy while he lives :
Let him proclaim the generous,   5
   and there will be no lack of givers.
By the teaching of Taliesin
   the bards greatly profit.
He will fall, when the people
   stop admiring him.   10
Witchery is wont to be his—
   the spoliation of Avagδu ;
And, by skill, he has brought
   a finish to poetry.
Gwion opens his mouth—   15
   an accident his song.
The Gwiδon kept the kettle
   boiling without lapse of fire ;
it could make the dead alive—
   a most difficult task.   20

19 Gwnaethei delideu, 21
er yn oes oeseu.

9 Y trwyth dy·ðyccawd,
o ðawn Wenðyð gwawd. 24

10 Neu·d amgar cŵyndawd,
namyn pwy i chyn·evawd?

11 Cy·meint cerð davawd
a dêlis ciwdawd. 28

12 Py·r na thraethwch, rhawg,
lad uch Ꝉyn Ꝉathrawd?

13 Penniꝉiach *rhoed* pawb—
dy·byð yna nawd.

14 *A*ð·wyn *da*tcan*i*ad; 33
neu·r ðoeth ostegiad.

15 Trwyðed, p*ei*r ynad
i varð a cheinad.

Tri ugein mlyneð, 37
16 yd bortheis lawrweð,
yn·ovr caw giwed,
yn elvyð Red*eg.*

17 Can gwŷs a·m dy·oeð;
Can rhi ynðun oeð;

18 can yw yð aethant 43
pan yw y doethant,
cân eilewyð gant,

19 ac a·u darogant.
Ꝉadon, verch Liant,

20 oeð bychan i chwant 48
o eur ac ariant.
Pwy·r byw ðy·adas

21 waed y·ar i gwynnglas?
Odid traethator;
mawr y molhator. 53

12

She had worked at metals   21
  from immemorial times.
She now brings a concoction
  of the gift of the goddess of song.
She dearly loves a festival—
  but what of the old custom ?   26
The community's pay being propor-
  tionate to the quantum of poetry,
  why do ye not, for a while, recite
  what is good over the sparkling li-
Let all *contribute* verses— ⌊quor ?
  the custom will then appear.   32
Pleasant was the recital ;
  then silence was proclaimed :
The Justiciar causes a licence (to
  be given) *to bard and minstrel.*   36

For three score years,
I have supported earthly form in
  the quarter of the licensed tribe,
  in the land of Red*eg.*   40
A hundred mansions I frequented ;
A hundred chiefs in them were ;
Since they have gone,
  whence they came,
  the minstrel shall sing of all,   45
  and prophesy concerning them.
Latona, daughter of the Ocean,
       had small desire
       for gold and silver.
What living person has shed   50
  blood on her sacred island ?
The fact has hardly been mentioned,
  though it is worthy of great praise.

19 Mi·d·wyv Daliessin:
Rhy·phrydav iawn ỻîn.
23 Parahav, hyd ffin,
yng·hyn·elw Elphin.
Neu·r *di*·deilynghed
24 o riv eur δlyed.
Pan gassâd, carad
anudon a brad.
25 Nu, neu·r chwenych vad,
trwy gyweg *avrllad*:
26 Go·gyv·archwy*v* vrawd.
Ni wyrthid an gwawd:
Ni wybyδ nebawd.
20 Doethur, priv gelvyδ,
dis·pwyỻawd sywyδ,
2 am wŷth edryvyδ—
doleu dynwedyδ.
3 A·m gŵyr gwawd gelvyδ:
Cerδwn Đuw yssyδ.
4 Drwy ieith Dalhaearn,
Bedyδ vuδ δyδ varn.
A varnwys deithi
5 angerδ varδoni,
Ev, o·i rin, roδes
awen ang·hy·mes.
6 Seith ugein ogrven
yssyδ yn awen:
7 ŵyth, o bob ugein,
yd vyδ yn un *sain*—
asswyn yn·i·wŷth;
8 asswyn yng·or·wŷth;
asswyn *oll* yssyδ.
9 Yn nev, uch elvyδ,
y mae a·u gwybyδ.

I am Taliesin—   54
I sing of true lineage.
I shall continue, to the end,
   in my pristine service of Elffin.
He was removed from among the
   number of the golden nobility.   59
When he was hated, loved were
   perjuries and treachery.
Now, he seeks relief
      from the fragile wafers.
      Let me call in a frate.
He will set no value on our praise :   65
   he will know no one.
The sage, foremost in skill,
   shall consult astrology,
   about the main line of descent—
   the links of the anthropologist.   70
      I know a fine psalm :
      Let us laud the Living God.
      By the teaching of Talhaearn,
      Baptism will help at the last.
He, who fixed the conditions   75
   of poetic frenzy,
   did, of his secret, impart
   inspiration without stint.
Seven score chords
   there are in music :   80
The octave of every score,
   which is ever in harmony,
   enchants in calm—
   enchants in storm—
   enchants all there is.   85
In heaven above there is One
   who knows the harmonies.

15

20 Py dristid yssyð   88
     well no ꞕewenyð?
     Go·gwn ðeðv rhadeu
11 awen, ban ðy·ffreu—
     am gelvyð dâleu—   92
     am ðedwyð ðïeu—
12 am vucheð ara
     oeseu escorva—
13 am hawl tëyrnva
     byhyd cyng·wala.   97
     Am gy·haval vy*d*,
14 *su*ðen trwy weryd.
     Mawrhydig sywyd !   100
15 Pan dy·gyv·rensid?
     Pan och awel gryd?
     Pan vyð go·hoew bryd?
16 Pan vyð môr hyvryd?
     Pan yw gwrð echen?   105
17 Pan echrëwyd nen?
     neu heul, pan ðodir?
     Pan yw töir tir?
18 Tô y tir, pwy i vaint?
     Pan tyvhid gwycheint?   110
19 Gwycheint pan dynnit?
     Pan yw gwrð gweryð?
20 Gweryd pan yw gwyrð?
     Pwy echenis gyrð?
21 Cyrð pwy echenwys?   115
     Ys·tir, ystyriwys,
     ystyrieid ꞕyvreu,
     cylch beirð, a·u cyvreu.
22 Ped vwynt yd ffreuynt ;
     ped ffreuynt yð ynt :   120

16

What sadness is there 88
 better than gladness?
I KNOW the law of the favours
 of the muse, when she gushes forth —
 about the artistic recompenses —
 about the happy days — 93
 about the quiet life
 of the ages to come —
 about the claim of the kingdom 96
 unto full fruition.
To obtain such a life, they
 must sink through the sod.

Majestic is knowledge! 100
Whence has it been imparted?
Whence the moan of the wind that stirs?
Whence the light of the countenance?
Whence is the sea pleasant?
Whence is the race vigorous? 105
Whence was created the firmament?
 or the sun, whence is it fixed?
Whence is clothed the land?
 covering the earth to what extent?
Whence grows its splendour? 110
Whence does its splendour attract?
Whence is youth ardent?
Whence is green the sod?
Who has sung the songs?
Whose song did he sing? 115
It is necessary, he considered,
 to study the books of the bards, their
 round, and all that pertains to them.
The *bards* bring forth what is in them;
 what they bring forth, that they are:

B 17

20 Beth a vont ar hynt,   121
23 *llyna* beth ydynt.
    Y ẟaear, pwy i ꝉed,
24   neu vaint i thewhed?
    Go·gwn drws*t* ꝉavnawr,   125
25   a m*ael* rhuẟ aml awr.
    Go·gwn a drevnawr,
    y·rhwng nev a ꝉawr.
26 Pan at·sein *go*·bant?
    Pan er·gyr di·vant?   130
21 Pan lewych ar·*v*ant?
    Pan vyẟ tywyꝉ nant?
    Anadl, pan yw du?
2 Pan yw creu avu?   134
    Bwch, pan yw bannawg?
3 Gwraig, pan yw serchawg?
    Llevrith, pan yw gwyn?
    Pan yw glas celyn?   138
4 Py·r b*re*varawt myn,
    yn ꝉïaws mehyn?
5 Pan yw barvawt *gwr*?
    Pan yw ceu evwr?   142
6 Pan yw meẟw Colŵyn?
    Pan yw ꝉeẟv *mor*ŵyn?
    Pan yw brith iyrchwyn?
7 Pan yw haꝉt halwyn?   146
    Cwrw, pan yw ystern?
8 Pan yw ꝉedruẟ gwern?
9 Pan yw rhuẟ egroes? —
    Nev wraig a·u dy·roes.   150
8 Pan yw gwyrẟ ꝉinos?
10 Pan ẟy·*gev*na nos,
    py ẟar·weir yssyẟ
    yn eur ꝉïant dyẟ!   154

18

What they are on tour,   121
  that is their true character.
The earth, what is its extent,
  or how great its thickness?
I know the clash of arms, and   125
  the ruddy work of constant shouting.
I know something of what is ordained
  twixt heaven and earth, (but)
Whence the echo of the hollow?
Whence the stroke of extinction?   130
Whence the brightness on the height?
Whence is the ravine ever in shadow?
The breath, whence is it foul?
Whence is the liver's blood?   134
The buck, whence is it antlered?
Woman, whence is she loving?
Milk, whence is it white?
Whence is green the holly?
Why does the kid bleat
  all over the place?   140
Whence is man bearded?
Whence is the cow-parsnip hollow?
Whence is the Calenian drunk?
Whence is a maiden gentle?
Whence is the roebuck spotted?   145
Whence is brine salty?
Beer, whence its ferment?
Whence the alder's reddish tinge?
Whence the ruddiness of hips? —
  Heaven's lady bestowed them.   150
Whence is green the linnet?
When the night retires,
  what wanton effulgence there is
  in the golden flood of day!   154

21 N*u*, *a* ŵyr neb pam   155
    y rhuδir bron huan,
12   yn lliw er·cyman?
    Newyδ an·aδ·wyn,
    tant telyn dy·gwyn.
13 Cog *yn ll*wyn py·*r* gan?   160
    py geidw yn δiδan?
14 P*w*y δwg *yng·*arthan
    gereint a·r arman?
    Py δy·δwg y glain
15   o er·δy·gnawd vein?   165
    Pan yw pêr erwein?
16 Pan yw gwyrliw brain?
    Talhaearn yssyδ
17   mwyhav sywedyδ :
    Ev am·gyffrawd wŷδ   170
    aches amod dyδ.
18 Go·gwn δa a drwg—
    cwδ â mownir vwg?
19 Mawr maint i o·gyhwg !
    Cawg pwy dy·livas?   175
20   Gwawr pwy gor·ffennas?
    Pwy a bregethas
    Eli ac Elias?
21 Go·gwn gogeu hav—
    a vyδant aeav?   180
    Awen a ganav,
22   o δwvn ys dy·gâv.
    Aw*e*n, cyd bei *v*ud,
    go·gwn i gor·*v*ryd.   184
23 Go·gwn ban δy·veinw ;
    Go·gwn ban δy·leinw?
24 Go·gwn ban δillyδ?
    Go·gwn ban wescryδ.   188

20

Now, does any one know why   155
  the sun's breast is crimsoned
  in pigment so perfect ?
Unpleasant news,   158
  the harp-string will bewail.
Why calls the Cuckoo in the grove ?
  what keeps it cheery ?
Who will bring into camp
  friends that make a great outcry ?   163
What brings the sparkle
  out of highly polished stones ?
Whence is perfumed the meadow-sweet ?
Whence is the greenish sheen of rooks ?
    Talhaiarn is the
      greatest seer :   169
    He comprehends the science of
      the approaching birth of day.
I know something of good and evil, (but)
  whither goes the smoke of green peat ?
Great the size of its curlings !
Whose bowl poured it forth ?   175
Whose dawn did it end ?
Whom did Eli and
  Elias declare ?
I know the summer cuckoos—
  do they live in winter ?   180
I shall sing of the muse, which
  I shall obtain from the abyss.
The muse, though it were mute,
I know its great impulses.   184
I know when it minishes ;
I know when it wells up ;
I know when it flows ;
I know when it overflows.   188

21 Go·gwn py begor   189
  25 yssyδ y·dan vor.
      Go·gwn eu heisorδ—
  26 pob un yn i oscorδ—
      Beth giglwyd yn·yδ,   193
22 bob dyδ ym·lwyδyn—
      Pob paladr yng·had—
  2 Pob dôs yng·hawad—   196
      Aδ·vwyn yd rann wawd ;
  3 nwy mevl go·gyffrawd.
      Aches gwŷδ gwyp*awd* :
  4 Go·gwn i nebawd.   200
      Py lenwis avon
      ar bobl Pharäon ?
  5 Py δy·δwg gŵyn*i*on—
      baran achwyson ?
  6 Py *oe*δ yscawl od*r*ev,   205
      ban δrychavwyd nev ?
      Pwy vu fforδ*r*ych hwy*r*,
  7 o δaer hyd awyr ?
      Pet bysseδ am peir,
      a·m amwyn neδeir.   210
  8 Pwy enw y δeu air
      ni eing yn un pair ?
  9 Pan yw mor meδwhawd ?
      Pan yw dil pyscawd ?   214
  10 mor vwy*n* vyδ eu cnawd,
      hyd ban yw meδysc.
  11 PAN YW gennawc pysc—
      du troed alarch gwyn— 218
  12 pelydrawg gwaew Ꝉym ?
      Ꝉwyth nev nid ystwng :
  13 Py bedeir echen
      ni wŷs eu gor·ffen ?   222

I know what motion   189
  there is beneath the sea.
I know the warp of the web,
  of every man in his clan —
What was heard during the day,
  every day in the year —   194
Every shaft in battle —
Every drop in a shower (—these I know).
Kindly will the muse apportion praise —
  she will not stir mischief.
The access of knowledge she knows :
  I know nothing.   200
What waters flowed
  over the people of Pharoah ?
Who will endure complaints —
  the rage of followers ?   204
What was the ladder's base,
  when it was raised towards heaven ?
Who was the evening's guide
  from earth to heaven ?   208
If it be fingers that fashion me,
  the hollow of the hand will shield me.
What name of two words
  will not *go* into any cauldron ?   212
Whence is the heaving of the sea ?
Whence is the structure of fish ?
How pleasant their " flesh "
  until it be tainted.   216
Whence is fish scaly ?   (Whence is)
  black, the foot of a white swan ?
Whence the gleaming of the sharp lance ?
Heaven's lineage is not abased :
Which are the four stocks
  which will know no end ?   222

22 *Gan nad* pwy vych, py·r grwydryδ?

15 A·th gyv·archav vargad *cyr*δ :
Gwr i·th gynnyδ ; escyn hynt !

16 Cuδ ynt a δên raeadr gwynt.
Traether vyng·oveg,   227

17   yn Evrev, yng·Roeg,
Lladin, a Chymraeg.

18   Lauda, laudate,
Jesu vab Jose.

Eilweith ym rhithad :—   232

19 Bum glas, bum gleisad ;
Bum ci, a bum hyδ ;

20 Bum iwrch y·mynyδ ;
Bum cyff, a bum rhaw ;   237

21 Bum bwell yn llaw ;
Bum ebill gevel,
vlwyδyn a hanner :

22 Bum ceilawg brithwyn,
ar ieir yn eδrin ;   242

23 Bum amws ar re ;
Bum tarw trostre ;

24 Bum rwch melinawr—
mâl ŷ(d a)maethawr.
Bum gronyn *yn·h*orgwys ;   247

25 *neu·m* tyvwys ym·ryn ;
Medawδ am dodawδ ;

26 Yn sawell gyrrawδ ;
Y·m rhuglawδ o law,   251

23 wrth vyng·o·δeivaw.
A·m harvolles iar
gravruδ, grib escar ;

2 Gor·ffwyseis naw nos,
yn i chroth yn was.   256

24

Whoever thou art, why dost thou wander ?
  I greet thee a student of arts :
A man to thy stature ; ascend in thy course.
Dark are what induce the rush of inspiration.
     Let my mind be set forth   227
     in Hebrew and Greek,
     Latin and Welsh.
     Praise thou, praise ye
     Jesus the son of Joseph.

Another time I was enchanted :—   232
I was a kingfisher ; I was a young salmon ;
I was a hound, and I was a hind ;
I was a buck on the mountain ;
I was a butt, and I was a spade ;   236
I was a hatchet in the hand ;
I was the pin of the tongs,
  for a year and a half.
I was a light-speckled cock   240
  over cackling hens.
I was the stallion of a stud :
I was the bull of a homestead :
I was the miller's bolter—   244
  the ground corn of the farmer.
I was a grain in the furrow's womb ;
I grew up on the hill ;
He, who sowed, reaped me ;   248
Into the kiln-pipe he drove me ;
He rubbed me out of hand,
  while he was scorching me.   251
There received me a hen,
  ruddy-clawed, with a divided comb ;
I rested nine nights
  in her womb a child.   255

25

23 Bum aδevedig ;   256
   Bum llad rhag gwledig.

 4 Bum marw ; bum *eisliw*—
   ceint yδ ym·eδiw.

   Bum *swyv* a·r waδawd— 260

 5 y·racδaw bum tawd.
   A·m eil gynghores,

 6 gras rhwyδ a·m rhoδes.
   Odid traethator ;

 7 Mawr y molhator.   265
   Mi·d·wyv Daliessin :
   Rhy·phrydav iawn llin.
   Parahav, hyd ffin,

 8 yng·hyn·elw Elffin.   270

Cad Godeu.

BUM yn llaws rhith,   1
  cyn bum dis·gyv·rith.

23 *Wyv clerwr* cwlvrith ;
   Credav *yng*·o·rith.   4

11 Bum dreigl yn awyr :
   Bum *yn* serwaw syr.

12 Bum gair yn llythyr :   8
   Bum llyvr i·m privder.

13 Bum llugyrn lleuver,
   vlwyδyn a hanner.

14 Bum bont, a·r driger
   ar drugein aber.   12
   Bum hynt ; bum eryr.

15 Bum corwg y·mŷr.
   Bum darweδ yn llad.

16 Bum dôs yng·hawad.   16

I was confessed ;   256
I was a wafer before the Gwledig.
I was dead ; I was a wraith.
I have sung of what I passed through.
I was the scum on the lees ;   260
Before that, I was yeast.

   He, a second time, counselled me,
    who gave me free grace.
   It scarcely can be told—   265
    greatly it will be praised.
     I am Taliesin
     I sing of true lineage.
     I will continue to the end   268
      in the pristine service of Elfin.

The Battle of the Scrub.

I Was in many a guise,   1
  before I was disenchanted.
I am a grey-cowled minstrel :
  I believe in illusion.
I was for a time in the sky :   5
  I was observing the stars.
I was a message in writing :
  I was a book to my priest.
I was the light of the altar-horns,
  for a year and a half.   10
I was a bridge, which is stationed
  over three score water-meets.
I went travelling : I was an eagle ;
  I was a coracle on the seas.
I was the attraction in good.   15
I was a drop in a shower.

Bum cleδyv yn anghad.   17
17 Bum yscwyd yng·hâd.
Bum tant yn·helyn
18 Iledrith, naw blwyδyn.   20
Yn·wvr *bum* ewyn.
Bum yspwng yn·hân.
19 Bum gwŷδ yng·warthan.
Nid un wyv ni gân ;   24
20 Ceint, er yn vychan,
yng·had godeu-vrig,
21 rhag Prydein wledig—
gwyδveirch *Gwy*δelig,   28
22 Ilynghes veueδig.
A gweint vil mawr em :
23 arnaw oeδ ganpen :
Ac hâd er·δygnawd,   32
dan vôn i davawd :
24 Hâd arall yssyδ,
yn i wegilyδ.
25 ILyffan du gavlaw*g* :   36
cant ewin arvaw*g*.
26 Y neidr vreith gribawg :
Eneid, drwy *i* phechawd,
a boenir yng·hnawd.   40
24 Bum y·Mevenyδ :
Cryssynt wellt a gwyδ :
2 Cenynt gerδorion :
Cyrchynt gadvaon :   44
3 Dadwyrein Vrython
a or*v*u Wydion.
4 Gelwyssid ar nevion,
ar Grist, a·i achwysson,   48
i δ*iffrid eu teyrnon,*
5 hyd ban y gwarettei

28

I was a sword in the hand-grip : 17
I was a shield in battle.
I was a string in the harp of
  enchantment for nine years. 20
In water I was the spume.
I was a sponge in the fire.
I was scrub in the covert. 23
I am not one who does not sing ;
  I sang, though I was little,
  at the battle of the Scrub-shoots,
  against Britain's Ruler
  and the *Irish* ships, 28
  a rich-laden fleet.
I s p e a r e d the bejewelled beast,
  which had a hundred heads ;
  with seed of great trouble 32
  under the root of his tongue ;
  and another seed
  at the base of his skull. 35
Also the cloven-footed black toad,
  armed with a hundred claws.
And the crested speckled snake—
  the soul, through *her* sin,
  will be punished in the flesh. 40
I was at Mevenyδ :
They hied to the reeds and woods ;
The minstrels played ;
The (men) rushed into battles.
The ascendancy of the Brython, 45
  bested Gwydion.
They called upon the saints,
  upon Christ, and his ministers, 48
to protect their princes
  until the Father, who had made them,

24 eu Rhi, rhwy·digonsei.   51
     As attebwys Dovyδ,
6 drwy iaith a·chelvyδ :
  "Rh*u*th*r*wch, rieδ gw*ŷ*δ,
     gantaw yn llüyδ,   55
7 i rwystraw pobl δig,
     ar law*r* anneδig.
8 Pan swynhwyd godeu,
     yng·o·*w*eith angheu,
     go·dorrid cadeu   60
9 o bedryd tanheu ;
     *c*wy*n*ynt am aereu—
10 trychyn drymδïeu.
     Dyar garδei bun,   64
     tarδei a·matgun—
11 blaen Ịin a blaen bun.
     Buδiant buch Anhun,
12 wn*a*ei ennilỊ i·n,   68
     yng·waed hyd a·n glin.

15 *Nu*, G w e r n, *ym*·laen Ịin,
     a want gysevin.
16 H e l y g a C h e r d i n   72
     buant hwy*r* i·r vyδin.
17 E i r i n w y δ yspin—
     an·whant o δynin—
     C e r i, cy·vrenhin,   76
18 gor·thrychan wrthrin.
     Ịf u o n w y δ eithid,
19 erbyn Ịu gwryd.
     A v a n w y δ wneith*p*wyd   80
20 yn oreu ym·wyd,
     er celwch bywyd,
     nid er nerthu gwyd.

would bring deliverance.   51
The Lord made answer
  by efficacious word :—
" Rush, ye chiefs of the wood,
  with the prince in your thousands,
to hinder envious people (coming) 56
  upon an inhabited region.
When the shrubs were enchanted
  for the work of destruction,
the engagements were interrupted 60
  by the harmony of the harps,
which deplored the conflicts,
  and banished sorrowful days.
Tumult drove away many, *but*   64
  brought out a noble chief — flower
of his line, and leader of the host.
The reward of Anthony's manner
  of life would do us good,   68
  in blood up to our knee.

Now, the Alders, at the head of the line,
  thrust forward, the first in time.
The Willows and Mountain Ash   72
  were late joining the army.
The Black thorns, full of spines —
  (how the child delights *in its fruit !*)
and their mate, the Medlar,
  will cut down all opposition.
The Rose marched along   78
  against a hero throng.
The Raspberry was decreed
  to serve most usefully as food,
for the sustenance of life —   82
  not to carry on strife.

31

24 R h o s w y δ a G w y δ v i d   84
    ac E i δ e w yr·bleðid.
    Mor E i t h n e n ergryd :
22 S i r i a n levyssid.
    B e d w, er i vawrvryd,   88
    hwyr y gwiscyssid ;
23 Nid er i lyvrder,
    namyn er i vawreδ.
24 E u r o n, delis bryd   92
    aΠmyr uch *g*wrhyd.
25 S e i n t w y δ, yng·hynteδ,
    cadeir gyng·wrysseδ.
26 O n n goreu dyrched,   96
    rhac bron tëyrned.
    ΙL w y v, er maraneδ,
25   ni oscöes droedveδ ;
    Ev Πaδei berveδ,   100
    eithav, a diweδ.
2 C o Π w y δ, bernyssid,
    wrth eiriv i arv-gryd.
3 G w y r o s, gwyn i vyd,   104
    tarw trin, tëyrn byd.
    Wrth vorawg voryd,
4 ΙF a w y δ ffyniessid.
    C e l y n glesyssid—   108
    bu ev yng·wrhyd.
5 Y s p y δ a d am·nâd ;
    haint ech yn anghad.
6 G w i n w y δ, gor·thöad,   112
    gor·thorsid yng·hâd—
    eu grawn an·rheithad.
7 B a n a d l, rhag bar cad,
    yn rhychva briwad.   116
8 E i t h i n ni bu vad :
    er hynn gwerinad.

The Wild Rose and the Woodbine 84
  with the Ivy intertwined.
How greatly the Poplar trembles,
  and the Cherry dares.
The Birch, for all its ambition,
  was tardily arrayed ;
Not from any diffidence, *but*   90
  because of its magnificence.
The Laburnum set its heart on the
  dingles rather than on bravery.
The Yew is to the fore,
  at the seat of war.   95
The Ash was exalted most
  before the sovereign power.
The Elm, despite vast numbers,
  swerved never a foot,
  but fell on the centre,   100
  on the wings, and the rear.
The H a z e l was esteemed,
  by its number in the quiver.
Hail, blessed C o r n e l t r e e,   104
  bull of battle, King of all.
By the channels of the sea,
  the B e e c h did prosperously.
The H o l l y livid grew,   108
  and manly acts he knew.
The W h i t e Thorn checked all—
  its virus aches in the palm.
The V i n e s, which roofed overhead,
  were cut down in battle,   113
  and their clusters plundered.
The B r o o m, before the rage of war,
  in the ditch lie broken.
The Gorse was never prized ;
  thus was it vulgarized.   118

25 Grug, buδyδ am·nad ;
dy werin swynad ;　　　　120
10　hy·dwyỻ erlyniad.
Rhac Derw buanawr
crynei nev a ỻawr.
11　Gelyn glew drussiawr,　　124
a·i enw ym·heuỻawr.
12　Craffus*r*wyδ cyngres,
cymraw a roδes.
Gwa*i*th *rhai*, gwrthodes ;　128
13　ereiỻ, go·dyỻes.
Por goreu, gormes,
14　ym·hlymnwyd mäes.
Go·ruthrawδ gynwyδ,　　132
aches veilonwyδ.
15　Castan, cewilyδ,
wrth rymiad Seinwyδ.

16　Handid du muchyδ ;　　136
Handid crwm mynyδ :
17　Handid cyl coedyδ :
Handid gwynt myr mawr—
18　er*g*an, cigleu r awr.　　140
A·n deiỻas *o* vedw :
A·n dad·rith, dad·edw :
19　A·n maglas blaen derw,
o warchan mael-derw.　144
20　Wherthinawg *cri* craig,
ne*b* nid ev tereig.

21　Nid o vam a thad,
pan y·m digonad.　　148
22　*Ys* crai y·m crëad,
o naw *elven*ad :

34

H e a t h ! that promotest obstruction,
  thy multitude has been enchanted :   120
  Easily ensnared, the pursuer.
Before the swift oak(-darts)
  heaven and earth did quake.
A brave enemy is spared,   124
  and his name preserved on a tablet.
The acuteness of his combination
  caused consternation.
The attack of some he refused ;
  others he riddled.   129
The foremost Prince doth give trouble
  in the conflict of the field.
He rushed the primeval wood,
  the passage of the mast trees.
The C h e s t n u t feeleth shame   134
  at the opposing power of the Y e w.

Black is sprung from jet,
  the hump from the mountain,
  the furnace from the woods,
  and great seas from the wind—
  he, who sings, has heard the roar.   140
We have emanated *from* birches :
He, who disenchants, will restore us.
Oak saplings ensnared us,
  by the incantation of the Oak-priest.
Full of laughter is the echo,   145
  which offends no man.

'Twas not of father and mother,
  whence I was born.
'Tis after a new fashion I was created
  from nine constituents :   150

25 O ffrwyth y ffrwytheu,   151
   y gwnaeth Duw ठechreu.
   o Vriaꝉ vlodeu ;
24 o vlawd gwŷठ-godeu—
25 *blawd Derw a* D y n a d,
   E r w e i n a B a n a d: 156
24 o Briठ y briठred :
25 o Đŵr tonn nawved :
   o Dan y lluched:
25 pan ym digoned.   160
26 A·m swynwys Vath *Hen,*
   cyn bum daearen.
26 A·m swynwys Wydion,
   mawr uठ *go*·rithion,   164
2 o eurvys Euron ;
   o *orne* mordon ;
   o bym *rhyw verthon—*
3 pymhwnt celvyठon.   168
   Archa*d*on, eil Math,
4 ban ym dygnawठ *i lath.*
   A·m swynwys Wledig,
5 ban vei loscedig.   172
   A·m swynwys sywyd
   sywyठon, cyn byd ;
6 ban vei genhyv vod ;
   ban ve*wn* vaint by*ch*od.   176
7 Harठ varठ, buठ a·n gnawd :
   yd veठav ar·wawd,
8 a draetho·m tavawd.
   Gwarieis yn ꝉychvor :   180
9 cysceis ym·Horffor.
   Neu b u m yn yscor,
   gan Dylan, eil mor :

36

From the essence of fruits   151
  did God begin :
  from Primrose flowers :
  from the pollen of shrubs —
  the pollen of Oak and Nettle,   155
  of Meadow-sweet and Broom ;
  from the Mould of the earth ;
  from the Water of the ninth wave ;
  from the Fire of the lightning —
  from these things was I made.   160
Math the Old enchanted me,
  before I was of the earth.
Gwydion, the great Master of
  phantoms, enchanted me
  from the Laburnum's golden finger ; 165
  from the breaker's prismatic hues ;
  from five kinds of loveliness —
  the five resources of wizards.
The fosterling of Math *was* chief lord
  when his wand afflicted me.   170
A Gwledig enchanted me,
  when he was being toasted.
The science of the astrologers
  enchanted me, before the world was ;
  when I drew the breath of life ;   175
  when I was a little thing.

Glorious bard, largess is ours :
I have a panegyric,
  which my tongue shall recite.
I played in the lagoons of the sea ; 180
  I slept at Pulford.
I was in the fortress
  with Dylan, fosterling of the sea.   183

26 Yng·hylch, ym·herveð,   184
    rhwng deu dëyrneð :

11 Yn ðeü waew an·chwant,
    o nev ban ðoethant.

12 Yn annwvn Ieuverant,   188
    wrth vrwydrin byðant.

13 Pedwar ugein cant,
    a weint er eu whant.

14 Nid ynt hŷn, na ieu,   192
    no mi yn eu bareu.

15 Arial canhwr a geni ;
    pawb anaw *cerð*, *eiðot ti*.

16 Cenhiv inheu i ng·hleðiv   196
    brith, *a wehynei* waed bri.

19 Ilachar i enw ; I<i>la</i>wn ffer,
    i luch, Iyw niver ;

20 ysceinynt i uvel,   200
    o ðovn yn uchel.

17 A·*i* darweð, Dovyð,
    o·*r* golo Ie byð :
    A·*i* oð*iv* Ilas baeð —   204

18 ev gwrith, ev dad·writh,
    yng·o·lith*r* deithoeð.

20 Bum neidr vraith ym·rynn :

21 Bum gwiber yn Iynn :   208
    Bum serw gan Gynbyn :

22 Bum bwystner ar hynn :
    Vyng·hassul a·m cawg,

23 armaav nid ynt dlawd :   212
    Pedrygant mw*lw*g

24 y·ar bawb a ðy·ðwg.
    Pym pennwn angheII
    a·m dal, a·m cym·heII :   216

On the borders, and at the centre,
  (I was) between two rulers.   185
(I was) two lustless lances,
  which came from heaven.
In the abyss they will scintillate ;
  a-fighting they will be.
Four score hundred   190
  I thrust for their pleasure.
They are neither older, nor
  younger, than I in their feuds.
Of the centurion's courage thou shalt sing :
Every gift of the muse is thine.   195
I myself will sing to my decorated
  sword, which spilled blood of renown.
Flaming his name ; highly tempered,
  his flashing guides the host :
  his sparks do spread   200
  from the low (earth) up high.
The Lord guides my sword,
  from His dwelling-place ;
By its stroke was slain the boar,
  which appears, and disappears,   205
  in his elusive journeyings.
I was a speckled snake on the hill ;
I was a dragon in the lake ;
I was the slave of Kynbyn ;
I was a herdsman besides.   210
My chasuble and chalice,
  I declare, are not trumperies :
A quarter per cent of the savings,
  from every one he will take.
Five flight-feathers of the wing   215
  support, and propel me :

26 Whyth march melynell,   217
    canweith yssyδ well :
26 Vy march, Melyngan,
    cyv·rêd a gwylan.
27 My·hun nid eban,   221
    cyv·rwng mor a glan.
 2 Neu gorwyv waedlan,
    ar naw can cynran.
 3 Rhuδ em vyng·hy*l*ch*r*wy ;   225
    Eur vyn yscwytrwy.
    Ni·m ganed yn adwy :
 4 A nu, y·m govwy,
    neb namyn Goronwy,   229
    o δol Edrywy.
 5 Hir wynn vym·ysawr :
    pell na bum heusawr.
 6 Treigleis y·mywn llawr,   233
    cyn bum llëenawr.
 7 Cylchyneis ynys ;
    cysceis *yng*·hann *gwys*,
 8 cant caer a·thrugus.   237
    Ðerwyδon doethur !
    drogenwch i Arthur.
 9 Yssid yssyδ hŷn ;
    neu·r vu ergenhym.   241
10 Ac un a δeryw
    O ystyr Dilyw,
    a Christ yn croccaw,
    a dyδbrawd rhac llaw.   245
11 Eurem yn er·wyll,
    a·m hudwy i berthyll ;
12 a byδiv drythyll,
    o armes lFeryll.   249

The staying power of an amber-coloured
  horse is a hundred times better :
Melyngan, my steed,
  keeps pace with the gull.   220
I myself shall not pass
  between sea and land.
(But) I am winning the battlefield
  against nine hundred warriors.
Ruby gemmed is my diadem ;   225
  Gold the rim of my shield.
I was not held in the pass :
  And now, save Goronwy,
  none will visit me
  from the mead of Edrywy.   230
Thin and white my fingers :
It is long since I was a herdsman.
I wandered in the earth,
  or ever I touched literature.
I circled the island :   235
  I slept in a hundred mansions,
    a hundred inhabited forts.
Ye learned druids !
  prophesy to Arthur.
There is what is older,   240
  of which we shall sing.
For instance, of what will happen
  in consequence of the Deluge,
  and of crucifying Christ,
  and of judgment to come.   245
The gold gem in darkness—
  may its beauty enchant me ;
  and let me be jubilant,
  because of Vergil's prophecy.   249

Mab gyvreu Taliessin.

CYV·ARCHAV Rëen   1
  i ystyriaw·m awen :
27 Pwy ðy·ðug i hanghen
  cyn no Cheridwen.
15 Cynhevin i·m byd   5
  a vu eisywyd :
  Myneich *ev* a leid !
16 *Gwy*byð, na·m dy·weid.
  Py·r na·m enregid   9
  un awr na·m erlid ?
17 Pwy ðodwy reith mwg ?
  Py·r echenir drwg ?
18 Py ffynhawn ðïwg   13
  argel tywyllwg ?
  Pan yw calav cann ?
19 Pan yw nos lloergan ?—
  arial ni chynnwyd,
  dy·yscwyd allan ?   18
20 Pan yw go·varvan
  twrv tonneu wrth lann ?
21 Er dyar dy·lann,
  dy ða haeð attam.   22
  Pan yw mor drwm maen ?
22 Pan yw mor llym draen ?
  a wðost pwy gwell,
23 a·i *gwaell*, a·i i vlaen ?   26
  Pwy beris barwyd,
  rhwng dyn ac annwyd ?
24 Pwy gwell yn aðwyd,
  a·i ieuanc, a·i llwyd ?   30

The Youth of Taliesin.

I WILL ask the Lord   1
  to consider my muse :
He sustained her need
  before the days of Ceridwen.
Familiar to my lot   5
  has poverty been :
The monks praise poverty !
  Know, there is no telling it me.
Why ! not one hour have I had
  without it persecuting me.   10
Who shall give a law to smoke ?
Why will evil be praised ?
What source can improve
  upon the canopy of night ?
Whence is white the reed ?   15
Whence the night's moonshine ?
(Whence) the splendour unkindled
  that shakes itself out ?
Whence the angry thunder of
  the waves against the shore ?   20
For all the tumult of the strand
  Thy goodness doth reach unto us.
Whence is stone so heavy ?
Whence is the thorn so prickly ?— 24
  Knowest thou which is sharper— .
  its point, or the *skewer's* ?
Who *first* raised a partition   27
  to protect man from the cold ?
In death, whose lot is the better,
  that of the young, or of the old ?

27 A ẃ𝛿ost beth wyd,   31
25 ban vych yn cyscwyd?—
   a·i corff, a·i eneid,
26 a·i angel canneid?   34
   Eilewy𝛿 celvy𝛿!
28 py·r na·m dy·wedy𝛿?
   A ẃ𝛿ost cw𝛿 vy𝛿   37
   nos yn aros dy𝛿?
2 A ẃ𝛿ost ar wŷ𝛿
   pet deilen yssy𝛿?
   Py 𝛿yrchis vyny𝛿,   41
3 cyn rhywiaw elvy𝛿?
   Py gynheil magwyr
4 daear, yn breswyl?
   Eneid! pwy i wyn*was*?   45
5 pwy gwelas? pwy gŵyr?
   Rhyve𝛿! yn llyvreu
6 nas gw𝛿an yn 𝛿iheu!
   Enioes—pwy i hadneu?   49
7 pwy pryd i haelodeu?
   Py barth pan 𝛿ineu
   rhy·wynt a rhy·ffreu?
8 Rhy·vel an·ygnawd,
   cadwr periglawd.   54
9 Rhyve𝛿av ar·wawd
   pan vu yng·wa𝛿awd.
   P*w*y goreu me𝛿dawd,
10 o ve𝛿 a bragawd?   58
   P*w*y goryw yn ffawd,
11 *n*amwyn Duw, *y* Drindawd?
   Py am*g*en draethawd,
12 traethwn o honawd?
   P*w*y peris ceinhawg   63
13 ariant, *yn* rhodawg?

44

Knowest thou what thou art,   31
  when thou art sleeping ?—
a body, or soul,
  or angel of light ?
Skilled minstrel !   35
  why wilt thou not answer me ?
Knowest thou where night
  awaits the day ?
Knowest thou, on a bush,   39
  how many leaves there be ?
What raised the mountain,
  before making the earth habitable ?
What supports the structure   43
  of the earth, for habitation ?
The Soul ! what is its blest abode ?
  who has seen it ? who knows it ?
Wonderful ! that in books   47
  they know not for certain.
Life ! who is its sponsor ?
  what the shape of its limbs ?
From what quarter pour forth
  hurricane and flood ?   52
A war, without utmost preparation,
  will endanger the soldier.
Most astonishing is the eulogy,
  that has sprung from the lees.   56
Who ordained drunkenness
  from mead and bragget ?
Who controls our destiny
  but God, the Trinity ?   60
What fitter utterance could
  I give concerning Thee ?
Who ordained the silver
  penny to be round ?   64

45

28 Pan yw rhedegawg,   65
   carr mor eichïawg?

14 Angheu, *ys* seiliawg;
   ym·hob gwlad, rhannawg.
   Awyr uch an pen,

15 ys ỻydan i ỻen: 70
   Uch nev nag *wybr*en,
   uch vyth yn Rheen.

16 Hynav ban anher,
   a ieu ieu, AMSER.

17 Yssid a bryder   75
   o·r bresent haeδ*er*.

18 Gwedy a·n rheuveδ
   py·r·n gwna byrhoedleδ?

19 Digawn ỻawrydeδ,
   cywestwch a beδ.   80
   A·r Gwr a·n *meithrin*

20 o·r wlad werthevin
   a·n duccwy *yn he*δ

21 attaw o·r diweδ.   84

Ꝧ Ꝧ Ꝧ

Cadeir Taliessin.

Ⓜ I·D·WYV merweryδ,   1
   Molawd Duw Ðovyδ:

31 Ỻwrw cyvranc cywyδ;
   cyvreu dyvnwedyδ.   4

23 Harδ bron sywedyδ,
   ban ad·leveryδ.

24 Awen, cwδ echwyδ,
   ar veinẏoeth veinδyδ?   8

46

Whence is the movement   65
  of a wain so squeaky?
Death is established;
  In every land, 'tis allotted.
The firmament over our head —
  wide is its canopy :   70
Heaven is higher than the sky ;
  still higher is our Lord.
Oldest at its birth, younger
  and younger grows TIME.
There are who fear the   75
  deserts of their present life.
  After endowing us,
  why make us short-lived ?
Humiliation enough is
  association with the grave.   80
And may He, who *succours* us
  from the sovereign land,
  bring us *in peace*
  to Himself at the last.   84

� ᛏ ᛏ

The Chair of Taliesin.

I AM the ecstasy   1
  in the praise of the Lord God :
I am the life of verse competition,
  and the inspiration of the orator.   4
Beautiful the presence of the prophet
  when thou art repeating (his teachings).
The afflatus, where does it drop,
  on a serenely fine day?   8

31 Beirð lavar, lug·ðe,   9
     eu gwawd; ni·m *tawr* gre:
26 Rh*w*ystrad, ar ystre,
     ystryw mawr mic·re.
32 Nid mi wyv gerð vud :   13
1   Cyvarchav veirð tud :
     Rhy·ebrwyðav ðrud :
2   Rhy·dalmav ehud :   16
     Du·hunav dremud :
3   Terwynn*av* volud.
     Nid mi wyv gerð vâs :
4   Cyvarchav veirð tras.   20
     Beth gwaðawl Jðas?
5   Dovn aig, iawn aðas !
     pwy am·lenwis gas ;
     pob camp ym·noethas.
6 Pan yw dïen gwlith ?   25
     Pan yw ꝉad gwenith ?
7 Gwenyn, *pwy y* go·lit*h*,
     o glyd ac ystor ?
     Py gelwy tra mor ?
8 *yn* eurbiben liw ?   30
     a ꝉeu arian gwiw ?
     a rhuðem ang·rawn ?
9 ac ewyn eigiawn ?
     Py ðy·vrys ffynhawn ?
10 Berwr, py i ry·ðawn ?   35
     Py gysswꝉt gwerin ?
11 Brecci, bonheð ꝉyn—
     aꝉweð ꝉwyr wehyn !
12 ꝉeðv ꝉonneð meðlyn.
     A sywion synhwyr,   40
     a sywyd am·lwyr
13 a ovrwy weð ŵyr.

The Bards, at dawn, recite   9
  their songs—I heed not the herd :
  their great plot for a row
  was defeated on the spot.
I am not, *as* a singer, mute—   13
  I salute the bards of the district :
  I speed the bold :
  I check the rash :   16
  I wake up the looker on :
  I make eulogy aglow.
I am not, *as* a singer, shallow—
  I salute the bards of the clan.   20
What should the lot of Judas be ?
The deep sea would be a fit retribution :
  He sated his hate, (and)
  every crookedness displayed.
Whence is dew pleasant ?   25
Whence is wheat a blessing ?
What attracts bees
  from shelter and store ?
What lies hidden beyond the sea ?
  (What) *in* the orpiment hue ?   30
  and in quick-silver's sheen ?
  and in the free-flashing ruby ?
  and in the foam of the sea ?
What hastens the spring ?
What is the virtue of water-cress ?   35
What will unite the people ?—
The nob among drinks is new beer,
  the key of universal good fellowship.
  Subdued is the cheer of mead.
    Both the sparks of wit,   40
    and thorough knowledge
    light up even a wry face.

D   49

32 Gwrth a ŵyr *Myrðin*,　43
14　a maⅡ an·oðyn ;
　　a gwaðawl tra ffin—
15　*y* corwg gwydrin.　46
　　Ar·Ⅱa*d* pererin
　　ynt : pybyr a phyg,
16　ac urðawl segrffyg ;
　　a Ⅱyseu meðyg,　50
　　eⅡ aⅡwy venffyg ;
17　*Blagur* a blodeu,
　　a gwðig bertheu ;
　　BriaⅡu *doleu ;*
18　Briwðeil *llawryveu,*　55
　　a blaen gwyð-godeu ;
　　A mael, a meueð,
19　ac aml ad·neueð ;
　　A gwin tal-cibeð,
20　o gwvein rosseð ;　60
　　A dwvn ðŵr echwyð—
21　dawn hy·liv Dovyð.
　　Nev bren, puvawr vyð ;
22　ffrwythlawn i gynnyð.
　　Rhed iâs berwidyð　65
23　oð·uch peir pum-wŷð ;
　　A Gwiawn avon
　　a ovrwy hinon,
24　a mel, a meiⅡon,
　　a meðgyrn *llawnion.*　70
25　Aðwynid Dragon,
　　a dawn derwyðon.　⊨

50

Myrðin shall know opposition,   43
  and the decay of the abyss ;
  and *for* dower, beyond the bourne,
  the coracle of glass.   46
The oblations of the pilgrim
  are : pepper and pitch,
  and worthy sacrifice ;
  and medicinal plants,   50
  which may confer benefit ;
Blossom and flowers,
  and hedge-row riches ;
The primrose *of the meads*,
  the bruised leaves *of the bay*,   55
  and the (flower-)tops of bushes ;
Also produce, and store,
  and frequent garnerings ;
  and cups brimful of wine,
  from conventual superfluity.   60
And the sacred water of baptism,
  the flowing gift of the Lord.
Heaven's tree, full of fruit will be ;
  prosperously it spreads.
The boilings of the cauldron   65
  of the five sciences will run over :
  (this overflow), Gwion's stream,
  will produce fine weather,
  white clover, and honey,
  and *brimming* mead-horns.   70
   The Dragon will pacify
   the vates with a gift.

II.

GOLYCHAV Gu-lŵyδ—
Ev arglwyδ pob echen :
33 Arbenhig torvoeδ,   75
yng·hÿoeδ am orδen.
3 Ceint, yn yspyδawd,
uch gwirawd av·lawen.
4 Ceint rhag meibon �Ιⅼŷr,
yn ebyr Henvelen.   80
Gweleis drais tryⱴar,
5 ac avar, ac anghen.
Yd lethrynt lavnawr,
6 ar bennawr discowen.
Ceint rhag uδ clodleu,   85
7 yn·oleu *glan* Havren—
rhag Brochvael Powys,
a garwys vy awen.
8 Ceint, y·mŵyn rodle,
ym·ore rhag Urien—   90
9 yn e*ch*wyδ, am a·n traed,
*y*δ *oe*δ gwaed ar·δïen.
Neu·d amug gadeir—
10 daeth o bair Ceridwen :
Hawδvryd vyn·havawd   95
11 yn aδawd gwawd Ogrven.

12 Gwawd offeren δ*wyⱴ*, rhwy δigones
ae*ro*n, a Ιⅼefrith, a gwlith, a mes.
13 Ystyriem yn Ιⅼwyr, cyn *h*wyr gyffes,
δyvod yn δiheu, angheu *yn* nesnes.   100
15 Ac o dud EnΙⅼi dy·bi a·n lles—
d*w*yreant Ιⅼongawr ar glawr aches.
16 Galwn ar y Gwr an digones,
a·n nothwy rhag gwyth *ty*lwyth ang·hes.

52

II.

I Worship the Dear Lord—   73
  the Lord of every race :
  The supreme leader of the hosts (I
worship) publicly, because of his majesty.
  I sang over the unfortunate
liquor at its spilling.   78
  I sang before the sons of Llŷr
at the water-meets of Henvelen.
  I witnessed malignant
oppression, and sorrow, and want.
  They polished their blades   83
on the shining helmets.
  I sang before a famous lord,
in the meads of Severn bank—
before the Brochvael of Powys,
who loved my muse.   88
  I sang, in a pleasance,
of a morning, before Urien—
  in the evening, about our feet,
was the blood of dire execution.   92
(Urien) defended the chair, which
  emanated from Keridwen's cauldron.
My tongue delights
  in Ogrven's treasury of song.   96

The praise of *divine* service has produced
  abundant fruit, and milk, and dew, and mast.
We should consider fully, before postponing confession,
  that death's certain approach draws daily nearer.
From the colony of Bardsey will come our good—
  boats will appear on the face of the ferry.   102
Let us call on Him who made us :
May He protect us from the wrath of foreign tribes :

33 Pan *ad·*alwer Von, dirion väes,   105
    gwyn eu byd wleiδon, Saeson ar dres.

19 Doδwyv Deganhwy, er am·rysson,
    ar Vaelgwn, vwyn*h*av o·r achwyson.
    Ellyngeis v·arglwyδ, yng·ŵyδ dëon,

21   Elphin, bendevig *bon*heδigion.   110
    Yssid i·m gadeir gyweir gysson ;
    hyd vrawd parahawd gan gerδorion.

23 Bum yng·had Godeu y·gan Wydion,
    a rithwys elvyδ *yr* elestron —   114

25 gan *vab Iwery*δ, yn Iwerδon ;
    Gweleis ban *losc*wyd Morδwyd Tylɫon.

27 Cigleu gyvarvod am gerδorion
    a Gwyδyl, dievyl δifferogion.

34 O Benrhyn *go·luch* hyd lych ILëon,   119

2 Cymry, *o* un vryd, gwrhyd wirion —
    gwared gym·ri*wed* yng·hymelri.

3 Tair ceneδl wythlawn, *an·*iawn deithi —
    Gwyδyl, a Brith*i*on, a *G*ermani,
    a wnahon δi·heδ, a dy·vysci.   124

5 Am dervyn Prydein, cain i threvi,
    ceint rhag tëyrneδ uch meδ lestri :

7 Yng·heinion dëon, a·u dy·roδi,
    a·n dw*g* ben sywed, ced ryverthi.   128

8 Kyweir vyng·hadeir yng·Haer Sidi :
    Nis plawδ haint heneint a vo ynδi.

10 Ys gŵyr Manawyd a Phryderi,   131
    tyrr orian a·dan *geul*an rhegδi ;

11 ac am i banneu, ffrydieu gweilgi.
    A ffynhawn ffrydlawn yssyδ achδi —

13 whêgach nor gwin gwyn y Ilyn ynδi.
    A gweδy·th iolav, Oruchav Ri,   136

41 cyn gweryd gorod, cymmod a mi. ◈

When he is recalled to Mon, pleasant land,   105
  blessed the inhabitants will be, Saxons sailing away.
I came to Deganwy for the sake of competing —
  to Maelgwn, gentlest of the courtiers.
I liberated my lord, in the presence of the gentry,
  Elffin, the prince of the nobles :   110
My chair is one of perfect harmony ; for ever
  it will endure, a possession of the minstrels.
I was at the battle of Godeu with Gwydion,
  who enchanted the elements of the sedges.
I was with Bran, (son of Iweryð), in Ireland :   115
  I was a witness to the burning of Morðwyd Tyllon.
I have heard of minstrels meeting with
  the Gwyðyl, the protectors of evil spirits.
From *Holy*head to the lagoons of *Chester*,   119
  the Kymry, unanimously, will champion the in-
nocent — will deliver those bruised in war.
Three irascible peoples of wicked propensities —
  the Gwyðyl, the Scotti, and the Northmen,   123
  do create disturbance and confusion.
Beyond the border of Prydein, and its sweet homes,
  I have sung before Kings over the mead cups :
At the feasts of the gentry, and their bounty-giving 127
  may great inspiration, the gift of the spirit, possess us.
Harmonious is my chair at the fort of the whirlpools :
Disease shall not strike down the old therein.
Manawyd and Pryderi know of the moaning   131
  that breaks out from a cave, in front of the fort ;
  and of the tossings of the sea around its heights.
There is also a plentiful spring close to it ;
  pleasanter than white wine is the drink therein.
And, lastly, I entreat Thee, Almighty Father !   136
  ere I go under the sod, be reconciled with me. ☙

Cadeir Teyrnon.

A REITH awdl eglur— 1
   Awen tra messur,
34 am gorδeu antur,
16   o echen Arthur.
  A·i ffon a·i aes ffur,   5
17   a·i rëon rechtyr,
   a·i ri rwyviadur,
18   a·i riv yscwthwyr,
   a·i gochl goch-assur,
19   *ev* ergyr dros vur ;   10
  Ev cadr cy·messur,
   ym·hlith goscorδ nug ;
20 Neu·s dug, o gawrvur,
   veirch gwelw go·strodur.
21 Tëyrnon, henur,   15
   heilyn bascadur—
22   trydyδ dwvn δoethur
   i *ladu* Arthur.
  Arthur vendigad
23   ar gerδ gyvaenad—   20
   ar·wyneb, yng·had,
24   or·vawr bystylad.
  Pwy, y tri chynweisad,
25   a werchedwis wlad ?
  Pwy, y tri chyvarwyδ,   25
26   a gedwis arwyδ—
   a δaw, wrth awyδ,
   erbyn eu harglwyδ ?
35 Bann rhinweδ rhodwyδ :
   Bann vyδ hynt hoeweδ :   30
 2 Bann corn cerδetrwyδ :

The Chair of Teyrnon.

HE declaims a luminous ode,   1
  inspired beyond measure,
  about the buffettings of adventure,
  like those of Arthur.   4
With his lance & his wary shield,
  with his active generals,
  and his sovereign prince,
  and his company of thrusters,
  and his purple cloak,   9
  he pushes forward over the wall :
He is judiciously bold
  among his agitated retinue.
He brought, from the great wall,
  creamy horses used to the saddle.
Teyrnon, the elder,   15
  waits upon his guests :
  he is the third deeply wise
  man to bless Arthur.

    Arthur was praised
     in song by all; (for)   20
     he would face in battle
     tremendous tumult.
Who were the three chief ministers,
  who kept guard over the country ?
    Who were the three leaders   25
     who observed the sign—
     who will come with zeal
     to meet their lord ?
High the merit of a fort in a wood :
Evident is the pursuit of mirth :   30
Loud is the horn of the hunt :

35 Bann biw wrth echwyδ: 32
 3 Bann gwir pan δiscleir—
   bannach pan leveir:
 4 Bann, pan δoeth o bair   35
   Ogrven awen dair.
   Bum mynawg my*gr*-eir
 5 yng·hor*v* anneδeir.
   Ni δyly gadeir,
 6 ni gadwo vyng·air —   40
   Cadeir ǥyniv glaer:
   Awen huawdl haer.
 7 Pwy enw y tair caer
   rhwng Ỻiant a Ỻaer?
 8 Nis gŵyr, ni vo taer,   45
   eisylid eu maer.
   Pedeir caer yssyδ
 9 yn·*hud* Powyssyδ.
   Rhïeu mor Weryδ !
10 Am nid vo, nid vyδ—   50
   Nid vyδ, am nid vo—
11 Ỻynghesawr a ffo.
   Tohid gwaneg gro;
   tra dy·lan dyppo.
12 Nac aiỻt, nac adon,   55
   na bron, na thyno,
   na rhynnawd godo,
   a·ch diffrid yno
13 rhag gwynt, ban sorho.
   Cadeir tëyrn vo !   60
14 celvyδ rhwy cadwo:
   cedwitor yng·hô.
   Ceisitor ce*n*ig
15 cedwyr coỻedig.   64

Lowing the cow at sundown :   32
Clear is truth when it shines—
  still more clear when it speaks.
When they emerged from the cauldron   35
  glorious were Ogrven's muses three.
I was the master of the grand style
  at the dividing line in the stewards' halls.
None will merit the chair
  who observes not my law—   40
  the glorious chair of the contest :
The muse of the eloquent is dogmatic.
What are the names of the three forts
  twixt flood-tide and ebb ?   44
Only the persistent can learn of
  the expulsion of their steward.
Four strongholds there are
  in the Powysian country.   48
Ye lords of the Irish sea !
  what may not be will not be—
It will not be because it may not be—
  Your fleets shall flee.   52
The wave will cover the shingle—
  beyond the very bank it will flow.
Nor villain, nor lord,
  nor hill-slope, nor plain,   56
  nor a considerable shelter,
  will protect you then
  from the tempest, when it rages.
The chair of a ruler be it ;   60
  Skilful (the bard) who shall hold it—
  It shall be kept in memory.
A ballad shall be attempted
  to the perished warriors.   64

35 Tebygav ᵭull dig,   65
    diva pendevig
16 o ᵭull di·wynnig.
    O leon lurig
17 dyrchavawd gwledig,
    terwynn, hynevig.   70
18 Briwhawd bragad vrig,
    breinawl, eisorig.
    Orig ym·er*w*in
19 am dervyn whevrin—
    ieith oeᵭ eᵭëin.   75
    Aches ffysciolin
20 mordwyeid merin—
    go·blant Saraphin.
21 Dogn dwvn di·werin ;
    Dy·ɫyngem Elphin.   80

🮱 🮱 🮱

Raᴠeir Reriᴠwen.

REEN, rhy·mawyr ditheu   1
  gyreiveint o·m careᵭeu.
23 Yn·eweint, ym·hylgeineu
   ɫewychawd vy ɫeuvereu.   4
25 Myn*nw*n hoedl viniawg va*l* ɫeu,
   a weleis yma gynheu :
26 Diweᵭ yn ɫechweᵭ *vu i* Leu :
   Bu wrᵭ i hwrᵭ yng·hadeu.   8
36 Avagᵭu, vy mab inheu,
   dedwyᵭ, Dovyᵭ rwy·goreu.
2 Yng·hyv·amrysson gerᵭeu,   11
   oeᵭ gweɫ i synhwyr no·r veu.

I deem it a savage custom   65
   to destroy a prince
   after a foul fashion.
Out of the mailèd legion   68
   will arise a Gwledig,
   brilliant, elderly.
He will smash the first of the clan,
the prescriptive, chosen (heir).   72
Shortly he will grow exasperated,
   because of the border harshness—
   the very language was passing away.
Swift the approach   76
   of the sea-rovers—
   the fosterlings of Saraphim.
   Grievous is the solitary dungeon ;
   We must set Elffin free.   80

🙟 🙟 🙟

The Chair of Kerixwen.

LORD, be thou mindful of   1
   forgiveness for my sins.
At midnight, and at cock-crow
   My lights shall shine.   4
I could wish for an adventurous life like
ILeu's, whom I saw here erstwhile.
He, in ILechweδ, met his end—
   eager had been his attack in battle.
Avagδu, my own son,   9
   discreet the Lord created him :
In the minstrel competitions
   his wit was superior to mine.   12

36 Celvyðav gwr a gigleu—   13

  4 Gwydion ab Don, dygn vertheu,
    a hudwys wraig o vlodeu,

  5 a ðy·ðug voch o Ðeheu.   16
    Can bu iðaw ðysc oreu,

  6 dyd i vryd i agor pletheu.
    Ev a rithwys orŵyðawd

  7 y·ar logawd *Pryderi* lys,   20
    ac en·weris gyvrwyeu.

  8 Pan varnher y cadeireu,
    ar·benhig uðun y veu ;

  9 Vyng·hadeir a beir ðeðvon,   24
    a·m areith drŷ·n awdl gysson.

10 Rhy·m·gelwir Cyvrwys yng·*lwys* lys Dôn—

11   mi, ac Euronwy, a *Thëyrnon.*

    Gweleis ymlað taer, yng·*Haer* IFrancon, 28

13 bryd pylgeint, rhwng Gwytheint a Gwydion.
    Dyvieu, yn geugant, yð aethant Von,

14   i geisaw n escud am hudolion.

15 Aranrod drem-glod, tra gwawr hinon ;   32
    Mwyhav gwarth, i marth, o barth Brithon.

16 Dy·vrys, am i Ilys, evnys avon ;
    Llynghes a·i hechrys ; gwrys wrth terra.

18 Gwenwyn i chyn·wŷd, cylch byd yð â.   36
    Nid wy ðy·weid geu, Ilyvreu Beda.

    Cadeir gedwidyð yssyð yma ;

20   hyd vrawd parahawd yn Europa.

    A·n rothwy, Drindawd !   40

21   drugareð ðyðbrawd ;
    a chardawd gwyrda. ⊨

The most artful man, of whom I have heard, is   13
  Gwydion, the son of Don : endless his resources.
    He enchanted a maid out of flowers,
      and brought pigs from the South.   16
    In virtue of his thorough training
      he delights in straightening tangles.
    He enchanted a number of horses
      within the precincts of *Pryderi*'s Court ;   20
    he also imitated saddles.

    When the chairs are compared,
      mine will lead them all—
      my chair will set the laws, and   24
      my speech will ever turn to poetry.
I am named Cunning in the fair court of Dôn—
  I, and Euronwy, and Tëyrnon.   27

I witnessed a persistent fight at *Caer* IFrancon
at cockcrow, twixt Gwytheint & Gwydion.
One Thursday, in particular, they went towards Mon
  to seek diligently for charms.   31

The glory of Aranrod's looks exceeds summer dawn :
Most disgraceful the harrying of her by the Scotti :
Enemies from the Menei rush round her court ;   34
a fleet terrifies her ; it menaces close to land.
The infection of her early passion will circle the globe :
The writings of Bede do not bear false witness.

    The Guardian's chair is this here ;   38
      till doom, in Europe, it will endure.

    May the Trinity grant us
      mercy on the day of judgment ;
      also, the charity of the nobility.   42

Barðð-gybreu Taliessin.

PRIV gyvarch gelvyð, pan ry·lëad?
   Pwy cynt, a·i towyll, a·i goleuad?
1 Neu Aðav, pan vu? pa i ðy·grëad?
3 neu y·dan dydwed, py·r y seilad?
4 A volĺei hon*n*yn, nis myn pwyĺad. 5
Yssyð bechadur am·nivereid,
5 coĺawd wlad nevwy, plwyv offereid.

    Bore vebin, dêl ;   8
    6 o·r g*w*ânont, ceir bel.
    A*r* Eingl Aĺwyðel
    gwnaont eu rhyvel.
    7 Pan ðaw nos, a dyð?   12
    Pan vyð ĺwyd eryr?
    8 Pan yw towyĺ nos?
    Pan yw gwyrð ĺinos?
    Mor, pan ðy·verwid?   16
    9 cwð â nis gwelid.
    Yssid deir ffynnawn
    y·mynyð se*r*iawn.
    10 Yssid Gaer gorchawn   20
    a·dan donn eigawn.
    11 Go·ry·th·gyvarchawr
    pwy enw y porthawr.
    12 Pwy vu beriglawr   24
    i vab Meir mwynvawr?
    Pa vesssur mwy*h*av
    13 a orug adav?
    Pwy vessur uffern?   28
    Pwy tewhed i ĺenn?
    14 Pwy ĺed i geneu?
    Pwy maint i en·ieineu?

Taliesin's Bardic Lore.

THE Seer's primal questioning, when was it answered ?
  Which came first, or darkness, or light ?   2
Or Adam, when was he ? of what was he created ?
Or under the sward, what was the foundation laid ?
He, who has accepted assertions, cares not for reasoning.
He who sins times without number will forfeit
  the heavenly country, the home of devotion.
    The striplings's morning, may it dawn ;   8
  If they use the spear, there will be trouble.
      Upon the Anglo-Irish of Tegeingl
        may they make their war.
      Whence come night and day ?   12
      Whence is brown the eagle ?
      Whence is dark the night ?
      Whence is green the linnet ?
      The sea, whence was it storm-tossed ?   16
      Whither it goes, no one has seen.
      There are three fountains
        on mount Serion.
      There is a towering fort   20
        under the wave of the sea.
      Thou wilt be much questioned,
        as to the name of the door-keeper.
      Who was the shriving priest   24
        of Mary's gracious son ?
      What was the greatest measuring
          done by hand ?
      Who will measure Inferno ?   28
      How thick is its covering ?
      How wide its entrance ?
      How great its degrees of cold ?

1 Neu vlaen gwyδ ffaliwm,   32
   py estwng mor grwm?
   neu py rinweδon
16 yssyδ yn eu bon?
   Nu, ILeu a Gwydion,   36
17 buant gelvyδion :
   neu·r wδant lyvrion,
   pa*n* wnant *ledrithion.*
18 Pan δaw nos lïant,   40
   pan vyδ yn·i·vant?
   Cwδ â nos rhag dyδ?
19 Pan δaw noswŷlyδ?
   Patria nostra ambulo,   44
20 gen*te*s in adiuvando :
   Tonans, simil*o* signum,
21 rogitans for*te cast*rum.
   Am·wibiwn *ni* am gymyδ—   48
22 Am·geisant *wy* δeu gelvyδ.
   Am Gaer, gerein a·dan δyδ
23 rhy·dynn eirch pwythwr δovyδ ;
   yn·ŵyviant ys ân yn *lluy*δ. 52
24 Caffwynt, yn δirdan,
   Gymry yn griδvan.
25 Provator eneid,
   rhag IIwyth eisyIIeid.   56
   Kymry briv δirieid—
26 rhann rhy·goII bwyeid.
   Gwae I hir ucheneid,
   a·s gwyar honneid.   60
27 Dy·δöent, gwarthvor,
   wyδveirch δi·ar vor,
28 *ar* Eingl yng·hyngor.   63

66

Or the leaders of the barberry bushes, 32
  why do they bend so archedly?
  or what are the medicaments
  which are in their stems?
Now, ILeu & Gwydion   36
  have been wizards;
  they know the (Sibylline) books,
  hence they practise enchantments.
Whence cometh the flood of darkness
  when it is in evanishment?   41
Whither doth night retire before day?
Whence cometh the eventide?
In our native land I wander,   44
  a-helping of the clans :
Thundering, I simulate a portent,
  eagerly inquiring for the strong fort.
(While) we wander about the coombs,
  they are seeking for two wizards.   49
The hubbub, at dawn, draws around the
  fort the ships of the shoe-making chief;
Wantonly they go, a great company. 52
     Far and wide, they find
      Wales in distress.
     The very soul has been tried
      by the wandering horde.   56
     Kymry's chief misfortune is
      the lost blessing of the mass.
     O misery! long the groaning,
      which bleeds persistently.   60
     There will come, athwart the sea,
      ships to the shore,
      unto the Angles in Council.   63

1 Gwelawr arwyδion   64
   gwynieith ar Saeson.
29 Claudus in Syon
   o rwyvanusson.   67
30 Byδhawt penn seiron
   rhag IFichti lewon—
   marini Brithion.   70
31 Rhy·δar·o·ganon
   am *v*edi hëon,
   am Havren avon.
32 *O* lad ffradyr cynna,   74
   masswy fissa mala—
   eu ffwyr ffinied. Sel*a*.
33 Dir·drinei tra oedei ;
   Creawdwr or·iol*ei* ;   78
34 ILu gentis diff*er*ei,
   go·s·pwy*ll*e*i*, go·δygn*ei*.
   Coδ*ei* *ev* oscorδ mur,
35 *a* gorvu a mein·δur.   82

Ꝺeu·r vum gan wyr celvyδon—
Math Hên, *a Lleu, a Gwydion*,
3 pan re*i*bwyd c*eu* elestron.   85
   Bum gan·hymδeith achwyson,
2 vlwyddyn yng·Haer Ovanhon.
   Wyv hên, wyv newyδ wyδon :
   wyv swyv, wyv synhwyr ceinon.
4 Dy·govi*av* δy·hen Vrithion—   90
   Gwyδyl, kyl δifferogion.
5 *Ys* meδud *a wna* meδwon.
   Wyv barδ—ni ri*n*av i ei*ll*on :
6 Wyv *ll*yw, wyv syw amrysson.   94

Signs of deliverance are seen   64
  on the part of the Saxons,
  who had been shut up in Sëon,
  by the dominating peoples.   67
The chief engineers shall act
  against the bold Picts,
  (and) the sea-roving Scotti.   70
They prophesy about
  reaping what they sow
  beyond the river Severn.
By the blessing of a very good frate
calamities, disunited, will die down—   75
their assault will be weakened. Alleluia.
He was in constant conflict while he lived ;
  The Creator he fervently worshipped ;
The host of the nation he defended,
  civilised it somewhat, and gently chided.   80
He harassed the guards of the wall,
  and conquered them with pointed steel.

I was with the wise men—
  Math the old, *and Lleu, and Gwydion*,   84
  when the hollow reeds were enchanted.
I was the companion of courtiers,
  for a year, in Caer Ovanhon.
I am the ancient, I am the modern lore ;   88
  I am the animation and the wit of feasts.
I remember well the ancient Scotti,
  (and) the Gwyδyl, defenders of the furnace.
It is drinking *which makes* the drunkard.   92
I am a bard, I will not prophesy to strangers :
  I am the leader, and the life of competition.

3 Ys hëi ar a hëi,   95
  er a hëi, nis medi.
7 Di·r ffradyr yn i ffradri,
  posveirδ bronrein a δyvi :
8 Aδevhont, uch meδ lestri,
  y *gw*nahont gam varδoni.   100
9 A geisont *ged*, nis deubi,
10 heb gyvreith, heb raith rhoδi ;
   a gwedy hynn, digoni
11 brithvyd, o v*r*yd dyvysci,   104
   na *da*, *na* heδwch, *ni·w bi.*
   Ervyn : *ot erchych* ni·th vi,
12 Rëen ry·mawyr weδi :
13 Rhag ing, rhy·m·gwares moli   108
   Brenhin gogoniant, a·*n* Rhi.
   A·m go·gyvarch un celvyδ :—
14 "A weleist, gadarn arglwyδ,   111
   δarogan B u δ i a n t U ffe r n ?—
   HIC NEMO   PROGENIEM."
16 Dillyngwy*d* torv *av·lawen*,
   per Domin*i* virtut*e*m :
   Eu caethnawd a *gow*yllis—   116
17 *Sic salvi* i*p*si . estis.
   A chyn bo un bai arnoch,
18 ter·wyn boch i Δuw diheu.   119
19 A chyn y mynhwyv i·m dervyn cleu,
   cyn del ewynvriw ar vyng·eneu,
20 cyn vyng·hyvalleu ar llatheu pren,
21 boed i·m heneid y da gy·veδeu. 123
   A·breiδ a·m dy·weid Πythyr Πyvreu
22 *vod* cystuδ gwedy gwely angheu.
   A·r sawl a gigleu vym·arδ gyvreu,
24 rhy·phrynwynt wlad nev, aδev goreu. Þ

70

You can sow what you will, 95
  for all you sow, you will not reap.
To the frate in the friary a troop
  of swollen-breasted bards do come.
They admit, over the mead cups, that
  they cultivate the muse irregularly. 100
They that seek a boon shall not have it,
  regardless of law, and the rule of giving ;
and they that seek thereafter to create
mischief, from sheer love of anarchy,
  shall have, nor presents, nor peace. 105
Supplicate : if you ask for what you cannot
  have, the Lord will bear in mind your prayer.
When hard pressed, I have found relief in
  worshipping the King of Glory, our Father.
An ingenious man greets me thus : 110
  " Hast thou seen, mighty master, the pro-
    phecy concerning the Gain of Hell ?—
  THERE, NO ONE (BEARS AN) OFFSPRING."
A miserable crowd was set free
  by the merit of the Lord, 115
  who dowered their bonded state—
  thus are ye yourselves *saved*.
And before ye have any failing,
  may ye be fervent to the true God.
And before I wish for a speedy end ; 120
  before I foam at the mouth ; and
before my association with the boards,
  may my soul enjoy the good festivals.
Scarcely do books tell me that there
  will be suffering after the bed of death. 125
And such as have heard my bardic lore,
  let them secure heaven, the happiest home. ⌐

71

Add·wyneu Taliessin.

AÐWYN rin, penyd *grin* yn rhy·red ;
arall aδ·wyn, pan vyδ dy·in·gwared.

8 Aδ·wyn meδ, nwy gomeδ o gyffred ;
23 arall aδ·wyn, y·am gyrn cyv·yved.   4
Aδ·wyn *warthegyδ*, Nuδ, *ar* breiδ nav ;
25 arall aδ·wyn, hael ŵyl o *luδ* hav.
Aδ·wyn aeron amser cynhaeav ;
arall aδ·wyn, gwenith ar galav.   8
27 Aδ·wyn heul yn *uchel* yn nwyvre ;
arall aδ·wyn, rhythaδ hwyr, a·i δe.
9 Aδ·wyn *amws* myng·vras y·mangre ;
2 arall aδ·wyn, march di·lyw, hŵë.   12
Aδ·wyn cant ac ariant am·aerwy ;
arall aδ·wyn, i vorwyn, modrwy.
4 Aδ·wyn cryr, ar lan Ilyr, ban Ilanhwy ;
arall aδ·wyn, gwylein yn gwarwy.   16
5 Aδ·wyn marchawg ac eurgalch gylchwy ;
arall aδ·wyn, aδ·wyn yn adwy.
Aδ·wyn Einawn, meδig i lïaws ;
7 arall aδ·wyn, ceIlawr hael, hynaws.   20
Aδ·wyn Mei i gogeu ac ëaws ;
arall aδwyn, pan vyδ hinon haws.
9 Aδ·wyn rhïein, a pherffeith neithawr ;
arall aδ·wyn, cyv·lwyn a garhawr.   24
Aδ·wyn bryd wrth benyd periglawr ;
11 arall aδ·wyn, dy δwyn yn aIlawr.
Aδ·wyn meδ yng·hynteδ i gerδawr ;
12 arall aδ·wyn, am dervyn torv vawr.   28
Aδ·wyn cleir catholig yn eglwys ;
arall aδ·wyn, hyneiv neuaδwys.

𝕿𝖍𝖊 𝖕𝖑𝖊𝖆𝖘𝖆𝖓𝖙 𝖙𝖍𝖎𝖓𝖌𝖘 𝖔𝖋 𝕿𝖆𝖑𝖎𝖊𝖘𝖎𝖓.

P LEASANT the feeling that penance kills excess ;
 pleasant, too, will be the hour of deliverance.
Pleasant is mead; none will refuse it with reason :
 Pleasant too around the horns to drink together. 4
Pleasant herdsman is Nuδ over the Lord's flock ;
 pleasant, too, a generous feast of the summer's
Pleasant are fruits in harvest time ; ⌊wealth.
 pleasant, too, is wheat on the stalk.   8
Pleasant is the sun on high in the sky ; p., too,
 is his looming large of an evening at his setting.
Fine is the long-maned stallion in the stud, 11
 and pleasant the horse that is quiet without a bit.
Pleasant is a bracelet and necklace of silver :
 pleasant, too, to a maid is a wedding ring. 14
Fair is the heron on the tidal reach at its
 flooding, & beautiful are the gulls at play.
Comely is the knight with gold-enamelled shield ;
 and blest is the merciful in the breach. 18
Pleasant is Einon, a physician to many ; pleasant,
 too, a generous, good-natured cellarer.
Pleasant is May to cuckoos and nightingales ;
 pleasant, too, when summer is more advanced. 22
Pleasant is a bride and a perfect wedding feast ;
 pleasing, too, is a betrothal to one that is loved.
Noble the resolution under the penance of the
 priest, and blest thine offering unto the altar. 26
Pleasant is mead, within the court, to the minstrel ;
 p., too, to be beyond the edge of a great crowd.
Delightful are the broad-minded clerics of a church,
 and pleasing the elders of an assembly. 30

73

8 Aδ·wyn plwyv cym·rwyv, Dwyv a'i towys ;
  arall aδ·wyn, amser paradwys.   32

15 Aδ·wyn Iloer, Ilewychawd yn elvyδ ;
  arall aδ·wyn pan da δy·m·govyδ.
  Aδ·wyn hav ac arav *hwyr* hirδyδ ;

17 arall aδwyn, a·threiδ a geryδ.   36
  Aδ·wyn blodeu ar warthav perwyδ ;
  arall aδ·wyn, a·chre cerenhyδ.

19 Aδ·wyn di·dryv *i* ewig ac eIein ;
  arall aδ·wyn, cynawr a·m harwein.   40

20 Aδ·wyn Iluarth, pan Ilwyδ i genhin ;
  arall aδ·wyn, cadavarth yn egin.

21 Aδ·wyn eδystr yng·hebystr Iledrin ;
  arall aδ·wyn, cyweithas brenhin.   44

23 Aδ·wyn glew, nwy go·leith go·gyweg ;
  arall aδ·wyn, *i* eIlein *gallineb*.

24 Aδ·wyn grug pan vytho ehöeg ;
  arall aδ·wyn, morva i wartheg.   48

25 Aδ·wyn dymhor, pan dynn Iloï laeth ;
  arall aδ·wyn, e*n*wyn maeronaeth.

26 Ac ys*sy*δ i mi aδ·wyn nid gwaeth,   51
  a·thal *llawn* vüal wrth dal meδweith.

27 Ad·wyn *i* bysc y Ilyn y Ilywiawd ;
10 arall aδ·wyn, gor·alw gwaryhawd.   54

2 Aδ·wyn gair a leveir y Drindawd ;
  arall aδ·wyn, penyd i bechawd.

3 *Ys* aδ·wynhav o bob aδ·wyndawd,
  caffel cerenhyδ Dovyδ δyδbrawd.   58

74

Delightful are a united people, God leading it ;
  delightful too the age of innocence.   32
Pleasant the moon that shines on earth ;
  pleasant, too, when the good you recall.
Pleasant is summer, & the lingering dusk of a long
  day ; pleasant, too, the communion thou lovest.   36
Beautiful are the flowers on the fruit-trees,
  and delightful the budding of friendship.
Pleasant is solitude to the roe and fawn ;
  pleasant, too, a huntsman to guide me.   40
Pleasant the garden when vegetables flourish ;
  and sweet the charlock in young corn.
Pleasant the charger that is bridled ;
  pleasant, too, the fellowship of a King.   44
Glorious the brave whom indecision will not destroy ;
  glorious, too, his splendid *circumspection*.
Pleasant the heath when it is green ;
  pleasant, too, the meadow to the cows.   48
Pleasant the season when calves draw milk ;
  pleasant, too, the butter-milk of the dairy.
  And what is to me no less pleasant,   51
  the guerdon of a full horn beside the mead-vat.
Pleasant to the fish the water he steers in :
  pleasant, too, to call decisively for the play.   54
Pleasant the message the Trinity delivers ;
  pleasant, too, (that there is) a penance for sin.
The pleasantest of every pleasant thing —
  the assured friendship of the Lord at the last.   58

Kanu Owein Gwyneð.

ꝶRIEN yr Echwyð,   1
    haelav ðyn bedyð!
57 ɪLïaws a roðyð,
15 i ðynion elvyð.   4
    Mal y cynuꝇyð,
16 yð *ad*·wesceryð.
    ɪLawen, beirð bedyð,
    tra vo dy vuchyð.   8
17 Ys mawr ꝇewenyð,
    gan glodvan, clod rhyð :
18 Ys mwy gogoniant—
    boð Urien, a·i blant.   12
    Ev yn arbennig,
    gor·uchel wledig—
    dinas peꝇennig—
    ceimad cyntëig.   16
    ɪLoegrwys a·i gwyðant,
    pan ym·adroðant.
    Angheu a gawsant,
    a mynych goðiant—   20
    ꝇosci eu trevred,
    a dwyn eu tuðed.
    Gorvlwng *o* goꝇed,
    a mawr ang·hyffred ;   24
    heb gaffel gwared
    rhag Urien Rheged.
    Rheged ðiffreidad,   27
    clodvawr angor gwlad !
    Boð yssyð arnad,
    o bob erglywad.   30

The praise of Owein Gwyneð.

URIEN, (lord) of the West,
  and most generous Christian !
Very many things thou givest
  to the men of the world.   4
As soon as thou gatherest,
  thou scatterest again.
Joyful, Christian bards will be,
  while thy life endures.   8
A great joy is liberal
  praise from the famed.
But greater glory is the
  favour of Urien & his sons.   12
He is our leader,
  and sovereign ruler — the
  strong shield of the stranger,
  and foremost champion.   16
The Ꝇoegrians shall know it,
  when they come to negotiate.
Slaughter they have suffered,
  and frequent tribulation :   20
  the burning of their homesteads,
  & the taking of their coat of mail.
Very sullen (are they),
  from loss and great hardship,   24
  without finding deliverance
  from Urien of Rheged.
Rheged's Protector, and   27
  glorious Anchor of the country !
Thou hast the good-will
  of every tongue that is heard.   30

77

Dwys dy beleidrad,
 ban ergyryδ gad.   32
58 Cad, ban δy·gyrchyδ,
 gwynieith a wneyδ.
 2 Tenid tei cyn dyδ,
 rhag uδ yr Echwyδ —   36
 3 yr Echwyδ teccav,
 a·i dynion haelav.
 Gnawd Eingl heb waesav
 4 am dëyrn glewhav,   40
 Glewhav eisiℓℓyδ —
 5 ti oreu yssyδ ;
 A vu, or a vyδ —
 6 ni·th oes gystedlyδ.   44
 Ban dremher arℓℓaw,
 ehelaeth dy braw :
 gnawd gwyleδ a *th*aw
 am dëyrn gognaw.   48
 Am·danat gwyr*th*eδ,
 ℓℓïaws maranheδ,
 Eurdëyrn Gogleδ —
 unben tëyrneδ.   52

Ͳ   Ͳ   Ͳ

Rhun aμ Owein Gwyneδ.

ᚤN i enw Ev,   wledig nev   or·chorδion,   1
 rhy·chanav,   rhy·chwynav   yn dragon.
64 Gwrthodes o·gyv·res gweryδon ;   3
 ℓℓïaws gryδ Run ab nuδ o lwyth Mon.
 2 Ni or·uchav cerδ beirδ   i o·verthon :
 Rhyveδ vael a ryδ hael lywyδon.   6

78

Serious are thy spear-thrusts,   31
  when instigating the fight :
  when thou enterest the list
  thou dost effect deliverance.
Houses were set on fire, ere dawn,   35
  from dread of the Lord of the West.
  The West is most fair,
  and her men most generous.   38
The Angles are habitually unreliable
  on behalf of a prince that is very brave.
Very brave are thy sons,
  but thou art the best.   42
Among those who were, or will be,
  thou hast not a peer.
Upon close observation,   45
  wide is thy experience ; (though)
  modesty and silence are usual
  about the activity of a prince.   48
Thou art clothed in virtues,
  like sand in number.
Thou art the golden ruler of Gogleδ,
  and supreme head of princes.   52

꙳ ꙳ ꙳

Elegy to Rhun, son of O. Gwyneδ.

IN His name, the Lord of Heaven's glorious   1
  company, I will extol, I will lament our leader.
He rejected the order of celibates ; the people
  sigh for Rhun, son of the lord of Mona's race.   4
The bards' art cannot over-exalt his fine gifts :
Wondrous the bounty which generous leaders bestow.

64 Un Ỻe—rhy·gethlyδ leithig—rhy·δlyav ;
4   rhy·chanav i wledig ;   8
     i wlad, tudwed er·grynig,
     nim gwel ; nis gwnav o·r newig.
6 An·hawδ wng dy·oỻwng ad·loneδ :
     Ev diffyg yn gwledig—ni orweδ :   12
     Edrychwn ad·wyth trwm uδ Gwyneδ ;
8 yn i vyw nis henyw buδ or beδ.
     Ni δygner a hoffer : wy buchynt
     galettach, aruthrach deith hael hynt.   16
10 Twrv pressen tra Phryden ry·phryder ;
     Go·hoew lurigawr a ry·lyccrer.
     A ry·tharvant lawr a ry·varnher :
12 Rhy·varn pawb, yng·wrthawd, ban glywher
     am yn ceimat yn ing nad ad·alwer.   21
     Nid ingwr di·law roed yn·aered,
14 namyn gwas graid i wrhyd a o·drawed.
     Ys eithawg o waỻawd yn Ỻywed,   24
     hwyr weδwid o belid ar·debed.
16 Ni ovyn i nebun a wnelher ;
     Nid i mi nac i chwi y dar·wetter.
     Tew vydav δiweδ hav nis cynnyδ,   28
18 namyn *awel yr oervel ai diffyδ.*
     Os Owein ni wyrein or newyδ,
     whegach *vyδ iδaw* genaw i henyδ.
19 Hweδleuawg drwyδedawg draethodyn—   32
     tëyrneδ yng·Wyneδ nwy *fferchyn.*
20 Meδ vâg, tebig heul hâv huenyδ,
     soneδ gan mwyhav. Ys cenhedyδ
     gân δoeth y·gan lwys veib eilassav.   36
22 Bint bydevi derw itti bryd hâv.
     Pryd mab Ỻëenawg am aeth buarth [tarth :
     am wawl, gwyn wawl Run : mal gwyn gnes
25 Tra gynnis, yδ enghis heb warchawd :   40

One place, the master-singer's seat, is my right ; 7
    I will sing to the Gwledig ;
   His country, a state perturbed,
   will not see me ; I cannot revive it.
It is a hard task to restore cheerfulness :
Our Ruler is failing ; he cannot rest. 12
Behold the heavy misfortune of Gwyneẟ's lord, who,
   in his day, will derive no comfort from the grave.
There is no tiring of the loved : *we* could wish for them
   the more arduous, more eventful journey of a long life.
The present turmoil, beyond Prydein, causes anxiety ;
   shining coats of mail will be tarnished.
They who disturb the country will be judged severely :
These all will condemn, when they hear 20
   of our champion's abiding distress.
It is no helpless stripling that was consigned to earth,
   but a youth, of ardent heroism, who had been smitten.
Dolorous from loss is our leader, who
   has been lately bereft of a radiant countenance. 25
He asks of no one what is being done ;
Neither to me nor to you does he speak much.
A crowded hive in autumn does not increase ;
   rather *the blast of the cold destroys it.*
If Owein cannot renew his vigour, dearer 30
   to him the whelp of his old stock becomes.
The gossipy, recitative verse of the roving bard
   the princes in Gwyneẟ would not honour.
As the sun promotes summer haze, so mead promotes
   chatter for the most part.   Thou permittest 35
   a wise lay by the serious sons of harmony.
Let them be as oak-swarms to thee in summer time.
The literateur will sing of the camp's sorrow—of the
   radiance, the bright radiance of Rhun : like the mist's
   luminous mantle, while rising, he disappeared unnoticed :

F

64 A chleδ cleδiva*d* i glevych*awd*.   41
26 Nid am·dyrr i *gedwyr* i ledrad,
   namyn yng·hyd ym·yscwyd y gy·wlad.
65 Rhy·dyIIyn, tal-*vriwyn* yscwydawr—   44
   rhactaleu, *bron-δoreu* y march*awr*.
2 O *garnial* drwst Morial *dy·chwelud* :
   Rhy·th·gar *IIu*, rhi-aIIu y Gwyn*dyd*.   47
3 Rhy·wystlan, gweinyδ*an* *yn* Goludawg,
   o G*lw*yd *ael* hyd *yng·*haer *veδ* Carawg.
   Ys dadl *h*ir Pen prys *d*ir : An·waIIawg
5 tĕyrneδ dewr *Wyn*eδ dangweδawg.   51

栄 栄 栄

Arδwyre Rheged.

AR·ÐWYRE Rheged, rhyseδ rhïeu,   1
ev it rhy·gostis, cyn *ni·s* bwy teu.
61 Gnissynt gad lavnawr, a chad vereu ;
3 Gwysynt wyr y·dan gylchwyawr ffleu,   4
   a chwyδyn yn gelein *rhag* yn martheu.
5 Ni mad vrwydrwyd rhi, ac ni·d mad geu ;
   yδ armerth gwledig wrth gym·ri*w*eu ;
   Neu·s gyrr i·w neges i geisadon.   8
7 Go·chawn varthawd mwth—moIIawd w*i*rion ;
   O dreig*l* dylaw*r* daw *a*dwytha*wl* donn.
9 Ni δoeth Wlff yn·hrais a·r *weis* i alon,
   oni δoeth Urien δyδ yn Aeron.   12
10 Nu, bu gyv·ergyr ; ni chymriwys
   dalgynawd Urien y·rag Powys :
11 Ni bu hy·vrwd bryd echen yrrwys.
   Hyveiδ a orδin, a·r IIu towys :   16

82

With the sword was smitten his dolour. 41
His warriors do not break loose into theft,
but, unitedly, they give the March a shaking.
They pierce, they shiver the edges of the shields ; the
frontlets, & breast-plates of the horses. From the 45
caracolling of the tumult of Morial thou hast returned.
The men of the Venedotian sovereign power love thee.
They pledge themselves to serve our prince, 48
from the Clwydian border to the grave-fort of Carawg.
Long disputed is the land of Penprys. Faultless
are the brave princes of peaceful Gwyneծ. 51

The Rising of Marchia.

THE rising of Marchia, the excess of its chiefs, 1
cost thee dearly, before it was thine.
They brandished the blades and spears of war :
They summoned, under the spreading shields, men 4
who fell dead before our blows. It *was*
impolitic to fight the sovereign, & *is* to be false,
(for) a ruler prepares retributive penalties :
He will send on his business the tax gatherers. 8
Quickly the blow will fall, even upon the innocent :
From the piling of taxes comes destruction.
*Ran*ulf did not molest his enemies,
until Urien, one day, arrived in Aeron. 12
Then there was a conflict, (but) it did not bruise
the uplifted front of Urien before Powys :
Nor was there enthusiasm about the men (R.) sent.
Hyveiծ presses forward, and leads the host : 16

61 *Nu*, dewr yw yn ym·ðeith taith gwyð *a*vwys :
   Di·vevl y dy·ðwyn *a gynllwynwys* :
14 Y·gan waed, Gwyðen *avon livwys.*
   Gweles Lwyvenyð ; *i h*uðyð gy·grŷn :   20
15   yn ði·oed ciliwyd yn eil vehyn.
   Câd, yn Rhyd ar Glwyd, gad ðy·vynner :
17 Câd, ge*r* llawr Brehyr, gad hir eurer :
   Câd, ym·hrysc *Alun*, gad *o*leui*r* :   24
   Câd, yn Aberi, oeð gyvranc ðir—
   briwed mawr gludwei*r* ; yng·weith Pen Coed,
20 llwyr y llithr cyn*ran* ar or·niant gwaed.
   Adveilaw *yna* wŷn gor·uchyd :   28
   Cyd mynnan Degeingl, eðyl wrthryd,
22 o ledruð gyvranc ac Wlff yn Rhyd.
   Gwell carher gwledig aned yn uð :
   Prydein ben-berchen brwysclawn *n*i byð :   32
24 neu·d ym·ðug ðillad, a glas *aes*awr,
   a cha*l*ch ehöeg wyg mor, *neu* lawr.
26 Ar·ðodes vorðwyd dros veirch Maelawr,
   o geneðl Voelyrch, *ynt* mor reidawl.   36
62 Hav y·dan aeav, arav yn llaw,
2 o red a roðwyd i·w harwylaw ;
   a gwest y·dan geirð i·w d*i·*wŷraw ;
   ac hyd orffen byð edrywyð caw.   40
4 Byðin yscub*awl*, dy·hawl *am* w*c*ð,
   am ðelw di·lëwr ; am leu*di*reð.
5 Myvi edrycheis *ar* weis rhag gwyð,
   peleidr ar yscwyð, yscwyd yn llaw—   44
7 Godeu a Rheged yn *cyd·*ðulliaw.
   Myvi a weleis wr—*ceis* ym·uarthawr—
   sarff virein vonheð, senghidyð lawr :
9 *Ev* go·ŵyr ryvel yð ar·gollawr,   48
   a·r maint a gollwyd yn argoedawr.

Bravely he adventures the pass of the woody ravines :
Without a hitch he carries out *his ambuscades :*
With blood *the streamlet* Gwyծen *flows.*
He came to ℟wyvenyծ ; *her* lords tremble, &   20
  straightway there was a retreat into another place.
There was, at Rhuծlan, a battle that will be cited :
There was, near the Baron's land, a battle that will be glorified :
There was, in the scrub of *Alun,* a battle that will be trumpeted.
There was, at the Abers, a calamitous event—a great   25
  flotilla was broken up : in the fight of Pen Coed
  a chief slips fatally on the profusion of blood.
Thereupon the *English* lust of supremacy dies away ;
  while their opponents insist on having Tegeingl   29
  after the gory enterprise with *Ran*ulf at the Ford.
More beloved is the ruler that was born a lord :
Prydein's over-lord is never reckless :   32
  He always bears mail, and *shield* of blue,
  and armour coloured like sea-weed, or grass.
  He casts his thigh over the steeds of Maelor
  of the Moelyrch breed : though so mettlesome,   36
  summer and winter, they are quiet to handle,
  because of the race-course provided to train them,
  and the whip-cord, in disgrace, to correct them :
  to the end this discipline will be evident.   40
The invading army clamours for a sight,
  for the presence of the destroyer, and for open lands.
I watched these men before the brake,
  with lances on shoulder, and shield in hand—   44
  I watched Godeu and Rheged marshalling together.
I saw the chief—observe him in the camps—
  a dragon of fine lineage, the trampler of the land.
He knows, now, something of the war that is lost,   48
  and the extent of the loss in the woods.

85

62 Minheu ym·or·wyth *vwythus* veδlyn,
11   gan Hy·veiδ hy·wr—hy·west δilyn.
  Ev ni·s cenhedis gyscawd gweithen,   52
13   δi threchu rhïeu, rhadeu ɪɪawen.
  Ys gwasaw*g* gwlad δa wrthvrwy*dr Urien.*

14   Oni vaɪɪwyv, yn hen,
      i·m dygn angheu anghen,   56
15   ni byδiv un δirwen
    oni volwyv Urien. ⊱

Cad Trwyn Moelvre . 1157.

Y̨N enw Gwledig nev, Goludawg—   1
    hy·drevnid vywyd cynheilwawg ;
29 Eirig i rethren rïeδawg ;
23 Rhïyδ gâr ryvel gor·herwawg.   4
  Ev differth aδ·vwyn lann ɪɪeinawg ;
25 a thorhid un hwch ardwyawg.

  Hil dy·chyvervyδ o vren*h*in—*a·i gym-*
26   *horth* o borth maw*r* Cerdin.   8
30 Ni chymeryn gyv·erbyn,
  Cyvoeth cyweithyδ Clydwyn.

2 Digonwyd, *ad*es y ɪɪynghes, o beleidr
  o blygheid bren *m*ês :   12
  Gwerinos a·u rhy·gyrches :
3 Prenial i bawb eu trachwres.

  Ang·hyvnein o gadeu δygnes Walɪawg :
  Gweɪɪ gwyδaw*g* nog aches.   16
5 Cadr a gyngres, o achles gwawd
  gognaw, *a* δivrawd δigones.

  Cad, ym·ro Trwyn *Moel*vre, drwy bres
7   marw*awl*, an·veidrawl y trancres.   20
8 Cadr a·u cym·r*iwh*wy, ganhawon !
  Cahad cad ; cryned yn Aeron.

Meanwhile *I* quaff freely the luxurious mead
 with Hyveið, the bold, who follows hospitality.
(Hyveið) never allows the shadow of war   52
 to damp the high spirits of his chiefs.
Subdued is the rich country that opposes Urien.

     Until I fall, in old age,
      into my dire, inevitable end,   56
      I shall have no pleasure
      but in the praise of Urien. ⹂

The Battle of Trwyn Moelvre.

IN the name of Heaven's puissant Ruler,   1
 (the Prince) orders an exemplary life ;
 Gleaming his commanding lance ;
 Our chief loves much-harrying war.   4
He defended the bonnie bank of ILeinawg ;
 and a protecting ship was destroyed.
He meets a king's descendant, with a host
      from the great port of Cerdin.   8
      These could not sustain the attack of
      the power of the chieftain Clydwyn.
Every man who left the fleet had his fill
      of darts, from the bent oak-bow—   12
 The common people rushed upon them :
 A shrine to all is ambition.
Loss of numbers by warfare afflicted Gwallawg.
      Better a bosky place than a roadstead.   16
      A strong combination, inspired by stirring
      ballads, destroys his plans.
In the dale, near Moelvre point, they fought through
      the deadly scrub—very long the death roll.
      The brave crush them, the dogs !   21
      After the battle there was trembling in Aeron.

30 Cad yn Arδunwen ; ac Aeron
10   eiδawed : Eured dy veibon ;   24
       Cad yng·hoed—beiδyδ boe*n* rhon,
11   δyδ ni veδylieist dy alon.
       Câd, yn rhag·wyδ, awr a Mabon :
12   Nid adrawδ ad·vrawd achubion.   28
13   Caer Wenvrewi ! ar·estwng *hon*
       Loegr saffwyawg i hav·*niveron*.
14 Câd, yn Rhos terra gan wawr, oeδ
       hwysc*lawn* : gwragawn yn wrawl.
15   Yn·echreu yng·heniad garw awr,   33
       rhïeu, o ryvel, rhy·δiffawr.
16 Gwŷr a oδev warth ingawg—Haearn-
17   *ei*δ a Hyveiδ, a Gwallawg.   36
18   Owein, o Vaelgyning δevawd,
       a wnaho beithwyr gorweiδawg.
19   Ym·Hen Coed, cleδyvein ;
           at·vyδ calaneδ gwain,   40
20   a brain ar δisperawd.
       Ym·Hrydein, yn Eiδin, yn aδevawg ; yng·
21   Avran, yn ad·van Brecheinawg.
22   Yn i erbyn, yn yscwn yn gaenawg,
       ni wyl *was*—ni welas Wallawg.   45

𝄞 𝄞 𝄞

𝔊𝔴𝔞𝔦𝔱𝔥 𝔏𝔩𝔴𝔶𝔟𝔢𝔦𝔫.

VORE δyw Sadwrn cad vawr a vu,   1
       or pan δwyre haul hyd i ge*v*nu.
60 Dy·gryswys IFlamδwyn yn bedwar llu :
       Godeu a Rheged yn *cyd*-δullu.   4
11 Dyvwy o Argoed hyd Arvynyδ :
12 ni cheffid aros hyd yr un dyδ.

88

(There was) a battle at Arδunwen, and Aeron was
    seized. Thy sons were covered with glory. 24
  In the woods, thou darest the lance's thrust :
  That day thou didst not mind thine enemies.

In the first brake there was a conflict with Mabon :
    Censure doth not mention the successes. 28
  The fort of Gwenvrewi—this doth humble
  England's pike-armed legions.

Then, at dawn, there was great havoc at Rhos
    y Cra : (the men) press forward bravely. 32
  At the first sound of the fierce warhoop,
  Chieftains, by combat, are snuffed out.

(Aye), heroes undergo the deathly shame—
    Haearneiδ, & Hyveiδ, & Gwallawg. 36
  Owein, from Maelconian habit,
  doth lay the intruders prostrate.

  At Pen Coed they fight with swords ;
  A time of lively carnage follows, 40
  with crows wheeling (overhead).

In Prydein, in Eiδin he is acknowledged (chief) ;
  also at Gavran on the Brecon border.
  Against him he will see no youth rising in a
  state of incrustation—he never saw Gwallawg. 45

ᚢ ᚢ ᚢ

The Battle of Llwyvein.

ONE Saturday morning there was a big battle, 1
   from the rising to the setting of the sun.
Flamδwyn made haste with four companies—
  Shropshire & the March marshall together.
He marches from Argoed to Arvynyδ, 5
  without a halt the whole day long.

60 Gor·elwis IFlamδwyn, vawr drebystawd,
13   a δoδynt yng·wystl—a ynt *w*arawd ?   8
14 Attebwys Owein, dir·wein ffossawd,
    na δoδynt, na·d ynt, na bint *w*arawd.
16 A theirei i vab *H*oel, bei gymwyawg
    lew, cyn a·s talei, o wystl, nebawd.   12
17 Gor·elwis Urien, uδ yr Echwyδ :—
    " O byδ gyvarvod am gerenhyδ,
18   "dyrchavwn eiδoed oδ·uch mynyδ —
19   "Cym·horthwn wyneb oδ·uch ymyl — 16
    " Dyrchavwn beleidr, uch-ben *mal* gwŷr,
21   "a chyrchwn IFlamδwyn yn i lüyδ,
    "a IIaδwn, ac ev a·i gyweithyδ."
22   A rhag gwaith ILwyvein   20
        bu IIawer celein ;
23   a·r *creu*, rhuδei vrain,
        rhag rhyvel gwyr*ein*.
24 Gwerin a gryswys gan or·nenyδ ;   24
    a rhinav, vlwyδyn, na·d wy gynnyδ.
25   Oni vaIIwyv, yn hen,
        i·m dygn angheu anghen,
26   ni byddiv un δir·wen
        oni volwyv Urien. Þ   29

Trawsganu Kynan Garwyn mab Brochvael.

CYNAN, cad δiffred,   1
    a·m ar·IIoves ged :
45 Cant ge*m* i·*m* o·δyged,
11   *y*·wrth or·gun trevred :   4
12 Cant gorwyδ, cyv·red,
    arian eu tuδed :

Flamðwyn, of mighty swagger, demanded aloud   7
  if they had come as hostages, & are submissive?
Owein, of cleaving stroke, answered that
  they had not—they neither do, nor will submit;   10
& his son, Hoel, vowed he would be shrived
  a hero, or ever he would give a single hostage.
(Then) Urien, Lord of the West, proclaimed aloud :—
"If there is to be an unfriendly meeting,   14
  "let us hoist our banner on the mountain top—
  "let us lift our eyes over the border—
  "let us, with spears overhead, like men
  "attack Flamðwyn among his host,   18
  "and kill, both him & his companions."

    And because of the Battle of Ilwyvein
      there was many a corse ;
      and *gore* crimsoned the crows   22
      before the raising of the war.
The people fled along the ravines, but I prophesy that, for a year, they will not prosper.

      Until I fall, in old age,   26
      into my dire, inevitable end,
      I shall take no pleasure,
      but in the praise of Urien.   29

A "Satire" on Rynan ap Owein Gwynedd.

RYNAN, the bulwark of battle,   1
  has bestowed benefits *on me :*
A hundred gems have been brought
  from the overlord of the province ;   4
A hundred horses, which run
  abreast, in silver trappings ;

45 Cant llenn ehöeg,
 o un gaen gyffred :   8
 Cant armell arved
14 a phym pwnt canted :
 Cleδyv—gwain galched—
15 Dwrn *mo*el, gwell honed. 12
 Cant cy*v*ranc, caffad ;
16 *pob* cas an·elwad.
 Cadelling ystrad
 *g*an gad yscogad.   16
17 Cad ar Wy, cyrched
 gwaewawr evrived.
 Gwenhwys a laδed
18 a llavn gwyarlled.   20
 Cad y·Mon vawrdeg,
 erglyd, a vroled.
19 Tra Menei myned,
 gwârwyd a orgred.   24
20 Cad yng·Hrûg Dyved —
 Aircol ar gerδed ;
21 ac ni ry·weled
 i viw, rhag ffriw neb.   28
 Mab Brochvael, broled
22 Dyved, i eiδuned.
 Cernyw cyvarched ;
23 ni mawl ieu dynghed.   32
 Dy·s·twg ang·hyffred,
 yn yδ a*n*·ialed.
24 Myg*r* cynnelw Cynan,
 cadeu ergyn*r*an.   36
25 A·i lew lavn llydan,
 cyv·wyrein vawrdan.
26 Cad yng·wlad Brachan,
 cadlan go·daran.   40

92

A hundred green tents, with every
  covering complete in one piece.   8
A hundred armlets, studded with
  five spikes in their rim-bands.
A sword—its scabbard had been enamell-
  ed, the handle was deemed better plain.
A hundred combats took place, &   13
  every enemy was confounded.
The Cadellian Strath
  by war was stirred.   16
Countless spearmen repaired
  to the battle on the Wye.
The Gwentians were slain
  by blood-dripping weapons.   20
A battle in Mon, the very fair
  and cosy *isle*, was vaunted.
While crossing the Menei, the rash
  were brought to their senses.   24
At the battle of Crûg Dyved,
  when Aircol was on his travels,
  the cows were not seen
  being driven away.   28
Let the son of Brochvael boast
  of Dyved (the object of) his desire.
Let him greet Cornwall, who
  will not praise the yoke of fate.   32
He undergoes hardship
  where (the land) has been laid waste.
Glorious the example of Kynan, who
  participates actively in battles.   36
And his brave, broad sword
  gives rise to a conflagration.
At the battle in the land of Brachan,
  the battlefield reverberates.   40

Tëyrneδ truan ! 41
46 crinynt rhag Cynan.
Ilywid yᵣ ymwan,
2 eisor Ilywethan 44
gynghein gymangan :
3 Nerthiad gwlad lydan.
Cigleu ymδiδan—
pawb yn eu cochvan, 48
4 cylch byd go·chwiban—
'Ceith ynt δi Gynan.'

簡 簡 簡

Daboltwch Urien.

LLYWYÐ e·chassav ; 1
Mi ni·w dir·mygav :
65 Urien a gyrchav,
7 iδaw yd ganav. 4
Pan δel vyng·waesav,
8 cynnwys a gaffav ;
a·r parth goreuhav,
y·dan eilassav. 8
9 Nuδ mawr y·m dawr byth—
i helyth a volav ;
10 neu·d av attaδunt,
ganthunt y byδav. 12
Neu chyrchav Ogleδ,
11 a·r mei dëyrneδ.
Cyn bei i·m lawreδ,
12 gwnelwn gyng·wystleδ. 16
Neu·d rhaid i·m hoffeδ—
Urien na·m gomeδ.

The wretched princes   41
  withered before Kynan.
He controls the fighting,
  as a piece of gut   44
  harmonizes the orchestra.
He is the stay of *England.*
I heard the talk of all
  in their gory beds :   48
Round the world it goes whispering :
The Captives are Cynan's.

য়   য়   য়

The Reconciliation with Urien.

THE Chief I do not dislike,   1
  nor do I disregard him.
To Urien I will go—
  to him will I sing.   4
When my warrant comes,
  I shall have abundance ;
  and that the best, under
  the influence of harmony.   8
For the great lord I ever care—
  his people I will praise :
I will go to them ;
  with them I will stay.   12
I will set out to Gogleð,
  and its territorial lords.
Before I go to my grave   15
  I would have an understanding :
I cannot live without friendship —
  Urien do not repel me.

13 ᴸᴸwyvenyδ direδ—
  ys meu eu rheuveδ—   20
  ys meu eu gwyl*ll*eδ—
14 ys meu eu ᴸᴸareδ—
  ys meu 'r delideu
  a·u gor·evrasseu.   24
15 *Cav* veδ o vual,
  a tha*l* di·eiseu,
  gan dëyrn goreu—
16 haelav rhy·gigleu.   28
  Tëyrned pob iaith
  it oᴸᴸ yδ ynt geith.
17 Rhagor, yd gŵynir,
  ys *h*ir dy o·leith.   32
18 Cyd ev mynasswn,
  gweu dyliv hen*dr*wm.
  Nid oeδ gweᴸᴸ gerwn,
19 cyn ni·s gwybyδwn :   36
  Weithon y gwelav
  y maint a garav.
20 Namyn er Duw uchav,
  ni·s di·ovry*d*av.   40
21 Dy dëyrn veibon—
  haelav dyn*i*adon,
  canant y hyscyrron,
22 yn·hireδ eu galon.   44
  Oni vaᴸᴸwyv, yn hen,
23 yn·ygn angheu anghen.
  ni byδiv un δir·wen
  oni volwyv Urien.   48

❀   ❀   ❀

The districts of ꟿwyvenyδ —   19
  mine their store —
  mine their wild places —
  mine their cultivated parts —
  mine their metals,
  and their produce rich.   24
I shall get mead in my horn,
  and gifts in abundance,
  from the best of princes —
  the most generous known.   28
The chiefs of every race
  to thee are all subjects.
Still, there is grief, because
  thy death is long deferred ;   32
  though I could wish to weave
  (for thee) the weft of extreme age.
There was none I loved better,
  though I knew it not ;   36
It is but now I find
  how great is my love.
Except for God, Most High,
  I will not renounce my love.   40
Thy princely sons are
  the most generous of men :
  their darts go whizzing
  into the lands of the enemy.   44
    Until I fall, in old age,
      into my dire, inevitable end,
      I shall take no pleasure,
      but in the praise of Urien. 48

꧁   ꧁   ꧁

Glaswawd Taliessin.

CENNADEU ᛞoᛞynt,   1
   mor·hynt anvonawg :
30 Dy·gawn i·n letcynt,
   mei*l*ynt yn ceudawd.   4
26 Gnawd rhwyv yn heli,
   beli *a·i* gwirawd.
31 Gnawd yscwyd yscawn
   yng·hamawn yscawd.   8

2 Gnawd gwyth ac adwyth o yspyᛞawd
   gaer : anav gant, maer mawrhawd :
   Ar Venei *ev* crai gyvlogawd ;
4 Mwy, ar Gonwy, gwynieith gwnahawd.   12

Ar oed, Ilwyth dy·reith anav barawd ;
6   o heyrn er·chwyrn eᛞyrn ᛞyrnawd.
Try·dyIlyn dra·chor, dorch dron, lüawg :
8 ILynghes yn aches, armes cyn brawd.   16

Tri diweᛞ yd gad am dri phriawd gwlad ;
9   Gwnahad b*r*ad *i* veᛞrawd :
Trin, o bop tu, rhy·phorthawd,
10 ac Eryri vre varnhawd.   20

ILu o Seis ac Ynt ᛞygn-awd yng·Hymry :
12 yᛞ erhy a weᛞwawd.
Rhag *Hywel, berwid llid brawd ;*
o varan tan·*re* tarᛞawd.

13 Cadwaladr a·i cwyn ;   25
   briwhawd bro*n* *o* vrwyn.
14 Gwellt Ilawr *an·rheithawd ;*
   a tho tei, tandawd.
15 At·vyᛞ rhyveᛞawd—
   gwr gan verch i vrawd.   30

The Lament of Taliesin.

THE envoys, sent on a
   sea expedition, have come :   1
We shall obtain news,
   which will sustain our hearts.   4
Oars are used to the sea —
   war will prove it true.
The shield is wont to be slight
   in the scathe of combat.   8

A thorn stockade commonly causes anger & hurt —
   a hundred inflictions its steward shall vaunt :
On the Menei he makes a fresh concord ;   11
What is more, on the Conwy, he effects deliverance.

In time, the clan will right the injury inflicted—
   with swift blades it will hail strokes :   ⌈cordon :
They broke through the outer circle, a vast, strong
The fleet in the roadstead is an omen of doom.

Three princes of the land met their ends —
   their betrayal led to the grave :   18
(Rhodri) supports the war on every side,
   and Eryri's height decides.

He afflicts the host of Saxons and Northmen
   in Wales ; their widows only are left.   22
Against *Hywel a brother's hatred seethes :*
Because of greed a conflagration springs up.

   Cadwaladr weeps for (Hywel),
     and breaks his heart from grief.
   He lays waste the cornfields,   27
     and fires the thatch of dwellings.
   There will appear a portent—
     an uncle will lie with his niece.   30

31 Dy·vynhyn diriawg,   31
   o lin Anarawd :
   O honaw, tyvhawd
17 coch gâd ry·bruδawd :
   nid arbed nebawd—
18 na chevnder na brawd.   36
   Wrth lev corn cadwr
   naw cant, yn avrδwl,
   o bedr-*or* δygnawd.
Dy gôv e*i*lw i l*o*esi*o*n o laswawd ;
ev rêd wrth a gawδ *d*y geudawd.   41

⚖ ⚖ ⚖

Canu y Meδδ.

Golychav Wledig pendevigva :   1
   Gwr a gynheil nev, Arglwyδ pob tra :
40 Gwr a wnaeth δ*iawd* i bawb yn δa ;
6 Gwr a wnaeth bob Ilad, ac a·i Ilwyδa.   4
7 Meδhed Maelgwn Von, ac a·n *llon*na
   o·i veδgorn ewyn, gwerlyn gwymha :
9 a·s cynnull gwenyn, ac ni·s mwynha.
   Meδ hidleid ! malid volud pob tra.   8
   Ilïaws creädur, a vâg terra,
11 a wnaeth Duw i δyn—*wy* ry·δonha :
   Rhai drud, a rhai mud, ev a·u mwynha.   11
   Rhai gwyllt, a rhai dôv—Dovyδ a·u gwna
13 yn vwyd*y*δ di·*dl*awd, hyd vrawd barha :
   Vu δiwig uδun, yn δillad yδ â.
14 Golychav Wledig, Pendevig heδ,
   i δillwng Elffin o alltudeδ :   16

They will call to account this terri-   31
  torial lord, of the line of Anarawd.
In consequence of this (sin) will follow
  the massacre that will make sad—
  which will spare no one,
  not even a cousin, or brother.   36
At the blare of the warrior's horn
  nine hundred, on all sides,
  will be sadly afflicted.
(My) dirge calls to mind thy sufferings,
  by going over what grieves thy heart.   41

ᚣ ᚣ ᚣ

The Mead-song.

I ADORE the King of the sovereign land ;   1
  Him, who supports heaven, the Lord of everything.
He made drink a blessing to all :
He made every good thing, & prospers it.   4
May Maelgwn be lord of Mon, & of what will cheer us
  out of his foaming mead-horn, the finest social drink.
The bees store, but they do not enjoy it :
Strained mead inspires the praise of everything.   8
The host of creatures, which the earth fosters,
  God made for man, for his welfare :
Some bold, & some timid, man enjoys them.
Some wild & some tame, God provides them   12
  for plenteous foods : this goes on for ever.
What was their covering will go into clothing.
I entreat the King, the prince of peace,
  to liberate Elffin from his exile :   16

16 Gwr a roðes i·m win, cwrw, a með,   17
   a meirch mawr modur, mirein eu gweð.
   A·m rhothwy etwa, mal *ced* ðiweð—
   wrth voð Duw, yn rhwyð, trwy enrhydeð,
   bym penhwn calan yng·hyman heð.
   Elffin, varchawg með, hwyr dy ogleð !   22

Canu y Cwrw.

ꟙENHYD TRAGYWYÐ ! 1
   Ys Tydi a we*h*yð
40 ðyliv nos a dyð—
24 Dyð i·m amodaw ;   4
   Nos i·m gorffwysaw :
25 Maleð ar·voꝇawr
   y·wrth Wledig mawr.
   Mawr Ðuw, digones   8
26 heul hav, a·i ry·wres :
   ac Ev ðigones
41 vuð coed a mäes.
   Galwer, yn aches,   12
   ar *i* eilig gymes.
2 *Gwŷl*, er pob neges,
   Dëws dy·m·gwares.
3 A chyn dybyð byd,   16
   a·i lwyth*eu* y*n* unvryd,
   ni *ve*ꝇynt ronyn
4 heb vaeth mechtëyrn.
   Ev a·i *s*awð yn ꝇyn,   20
5 oni vo egin :

Him, who gave me wine, beer, and mead,　　　17
　and big spirited horses in fine condition.
May he grant me further, as a final favour,
　by the grace of God, freely, & for honour's sake,
five times five new years of unbroken amity.　21
　　　Elffin, Knight of the mead, late be
　　　　thy Northerning.

＊　＊　＊

The Beer-song.

ETERNAL MIND !　　　　　　1
　　't is Thou that weavest
　the warp of night & day :
The day for my activities —　　　4
　the night for my rest.
Renewed life, *too*, comes
　from the Sovereign Ruler,
Who created the summer sun,　　8
　with its great heat ;
And ordained the
　produce of field & forest.
Call, in the haven,　　　　12
　upon His flowing justice.
See ! despite every transaction,
　God hath delivered me.
Though the nations of the earth　16
　were on one purpose bent,
　they could not convert one grain
　to malt, without the Lord's fosterage.
The Lord submerges it under
　water, until it be all sprouted :　21

41 A sawꝺ waith araỻ,   32
  oni vo   yn vaỻ.

6 Drewdawd dy·ꝺervyꝺ—
  ys gor·wag 'r elvyꝺ.   25

7 Golcher y ỻestri—
  byꝺ groew y brecci.

8 Pan vo arianeỻ,   28
  dy·ꝺyccer o geỻ—
  dyccer rhag rhïeu

9 i gain gyveꝺeu ;
  Nis gwrthryn neb deu ;   32
  y *grawn* a·i goreu.

10 Duw envyn i noꝺ ;
  yd vyꝺ *wrth* i voꝺ :

16 *I* deithi edmygant ;   36
  yn dry·*l*yvn carant.

17 Gaỻawr, goỻyng*ant*—
  go·*dorrant* an·chwant.
  Sy bwl symudant,   40
18 ban or·ꝺiwel tant.

26 Pwy a dal y ceinon ?—
  aeth Maelgwn o Von.

42 Ev cyrch, cerꝺorion,   44
3 seꝺ syberw Sëon.

10 Cant calan *l*onnwys :
  Cant car a·i hyvwys.

41 Gor·wyth meꝺw, meꝺwhawd,
11 o vynud pyscawd.   49

10 ỻariav yw Trindawd :
14 Hi i hun a·m gwarawd.

15 Ni ꝺigonir nebawd,
  heb gyfoeth y Drindawd.   53

He submerges it again   22
  until it be all sodden.
The offensive smell will cease—
  He will expel that element.
Let the vessels be cleansed,   26
  and the wort will be clear.
When the (beer) sparkles brightly,
  let it be brought from the cellar,   29
  & its fine entertaining qualities
  be placed before princes.
No couple will refuse it ;   32
  it is derived from grain.
God gave grain its sap,
  which pleases Him well ;
And men like its properties,   36
  which are loved extra mild :
They bring relaxation of the ener-
  gies, and satisfy strong desire :
  they banish dullness,   40
  when the strings pour forth.
Who will draw the first drinks,
  (now that) Maelgwn has left Mona ?
Minstrels will repair to the   44
  Court of the lord of Seiont.
Beer has cheered 100 new year (feasts) ;
  a hundred friends have toasted it.
  It is drinking like a fish   48
  that makes the drunkard.
    Most gracious is the Trinity,
    which will deliver me :
    None will be satisfied
      without its bounty.   53

Canu Urien.

· **Y**NG·OR Bowys,   1
   cân rhy·chedwys.
58 Parch, a chynnwys,
   a meδ veδwys.   5
15 Meueδwys veδ,
   e*r g*or·voleδ ;
   a chain direδ
   i mi yn rhe*u*veδ ;   8
16 a rhy*ss*eδ mawr
   o eur ogawr ;
   *Mil*awr a ched
17 a gyv·rived ;   12
   a·r cyvriviant
   a dor*r*ei whant :
17 A·*m* whant roδi
   er vy Ꝉochi —   16
   yd lad, yd grûg ;
19 yd vâg, yd vûg ;
   yd vûg, yd vâg,
   yd lad yn rhag.   20
20 Rhagweδ rothid
   i veirδ y byd.
   Be*ir*δ, yn geugant,
21 it yd weδant.
   Wrth *i* ewyꝉis,   25
   Duw rhy·th·beris
22 yn rihyδ gwys,
   rhag ovn dy·brys—
   annogiad cad—
23 diffreidiad gwlad ;   30

In praise of Urien.

IN the border of Powys,   1
  the muse he maintained.
Respect and plenty,
  and mead were his.   4
He stored mead
  for great rejoicings ;
And held fair lands
  for my welfare,   8
  with great abundance
  of golden crops.
Beasts, and gifts
  were counted out ;   12
  and the counting
  satisfied desire.
My wants thou suppliest,
  in order to cherish me :   16
Thy bounty blesses & increases :
  It breeds and lows,
  and lows and breeds,
  and blesses for ever.   20
Thou didst countenance
  the bards of the world :
The *bards*, assuredly,
  will do thee homage.   24
Agreeably to his will
  hath God raised thee,
  to be a ruler of a people
  against sudden panic—   28
  to be the stimulator of battle,
  and the country's defence.

58 Gwlad ծiffreidad ;   31
24 Cad annodad.
 Gnawd am danad,
 twrw pystylad :
25 pystylad dwrw,
 ac yved cwrw.   36
 Cwrw i·w yved,
26 a chain drevred,
 a *m*ain duծed
 rhy·m·an·ꝉoved.   40
59 ꝉwyvenyծ vann,
 ac eirch*eid* lann,
 yn un, trigan.
2 *Am* vawr a bychan, 44
 mi, Taliessin gan.
 Ys ti a·*m* diծan,
3 a thi, y goreu,
 o·r a gigleu,   48
 y*ng*·wrh*yd*r*eu.
 Molav inheu
4 dy weithredeu.
 Oni vaꝉwyf, yn hên, 52
5 i·m dygn angheu anghen,
 ni byծiv un ծirwen,
6 oni volwyv Urien. 55

II.

AC yr un vlyneծ,   1
 y bu i·n ծar·wꝉeծ.
59 Gwin am·haꝉ a meծ—
8 gw*er*hid ծi·*g*aseծ. 4

The country has been defended, and the war ended.   32
Usually, there is around thee
  the noise of prancing:
  the noise of dancing,
  and of drinking beer.   36
Beer for drinking,
  a beautiful homestead,
  and fine clothing—
  these were bestowed on me. 40
ℒwyvenyδ's height,
  & the suppliants' court
  are situated together.
Of great and small,   44
  I, Taliesin sing.
Thou dost spoil me:
  and, of all I have heard,
  thou art the best   48
  in deeds of valour.
Then will I praise
  thine actions.
Until I fall, in old age,   52
  into my dire, inevitable end,
  I shall take no pleasure,
  but in the praise of Urien. 55

II.

AND the same year   1
  we had a great feast.
  Plenteous wine and mead
  do allay animosity.   4

59 Ac *aer*wyr Godeu   5
 9 a heidant vereu,
   a·u penff*est*ineu,
   yn·hêg wyδväeu :   8
10 *Mal* el*hont* ae*l*wyd,
   δyffynt ym·hlymnwyd :
11 Pawb, a·i varch danaw,
   yn mynaw Godeu.   12
12 Achwaneg, anaw
   vuδ am li, am law.
   Wyth ugein, ụn ỻiw,
13 o loï a biw :   16
   Biw blith ac ychen
   a phob cain amgen.
14 Ni byδwn lawen,
   bei ỻëas Urien.   20
   Ys cu, cyn eithid
15 eis cryn*ion* o grŷd.
   Briger wen loched ;
16 Elor ry·δyged ;   24
   a gran gwyarỻed,
17 a·m gŵyr, go·noδed.
   Ang·wr byrr-b*w*yỻig
   vei, a weδw*ei i* wraig.   28
18 A·m ŷ*v* gwin ffeleig ;
   a·m ŷs myn gyỻ*eig*—
   w*y* a·m porth, a·m p*ra*in.
19 A·m syrth cyv·wyrein,   32
   cyn na phar gym*ein.*
   Tawav. Was *Wrwst !*
21 gwarandaw py drwst—
   a·i daear a grŷn,
   a·i mor a δir·dyn ?   37

Hence the warriors of Godeu   5
  pile up their spears,
  and their helmets,
  in the fair watch-towers :   8
So that those, who had come
  into the conflict, may go home.
Every one, with his horse
  under him, reaches Godeu.   12
Moreover, the minstrel gains
  by reason of rain & flood.
Eight score, all of a colour,
  of calves and cows—   16
  milch cows and oxen,
  and every fair thing besides.
(Still) I could not rejoice,
  were Urien slain.   20
He was beloved, before the round
  darts were sped from a quiver.
His white hair was spared :
  the litter was brought ;   24
  and his gory cheek,
  I trow, was protected.
He would be a witless recreant,
  should he put away his wife.   28
I drink the wine of a shrewd leader ;
  I eat the kid of the stag—
  these feed and feast me.
Elation befalls me,   32
  though it will not last long.
I will say no more.   Servant of
  Gwrwst, listen ! what *is* the noise ?
  Is it the earth trembling ?
  or, is the sea convulsed ?   37

59 Dy·wyn 'yng·hyn·gar,   38
  wrth i be*leitral.*
23 Ossid uch ym·ryn,
  neu·d Urien a·i grym.
  Ossid uch ym·hant,
24   neu·d Urien a·i gwant.   43
  Ossid uch y·mynyδ,
25   neu·d Urien a orvyδ.
  Ossid uch yn rhiw,
26   neu·d Urien a vriw.
  Ossid uch yng·Hlawδ,   48
  neu·d Urien a blawδ.
60 *Ar* hynt, *ac yng·hl*as,
  ym·hob cam uchas.
2 Nac un traw, na dau,   52
  ni nawd i·r angheu.
3 Ni byδ ar newyn,
  a phraiδ o·i gylchyn.
  *Yng·oror Ger*iawg,   56
4   gor·*lei*sawg lavar,
  Eil Angheu y pâr——
  y*d* laδ*ei* i escar.
  Oni vaⅡwyv, yn hen,   60
  i·m dygn angheu anghen,
  ni byδiv un δirwen,
  oni volwyv Urien.   ⟩   63

Papeil Taliessin.   Canu Urien.

◊YNG·WRHYD, go·gyv·*id* yn·hrafferth :   1
  O gwaedwyv, a weⅡwyv yn *gyd·n*erth ?
62 Gwir, gweleis rhag neb *drais*—ni·m gwa*r*es.
19 Pob annŵys, ev δimŵys vy·neges.   4

It is my old friend who shines forth
  by the light of his spear-thrusts. 39
If there be groaning on the hill,
  it is Urien who gives it volume.
If there be groaning in the dale, 42
  it is Urien who has thrusted.
If there be groaning on the mountain,
  it is Urien who is overcoming. 45
If there be groaning in a steep place,
  it is Urien who is wounding.
If there be groaning in the Dyke, 48
  it is Urien who is smiting.
On the march *and in camp*,
  at every step he prevailed.
An expedition, or two 52
  are not usually fatal :
And he will not starve
  with a flock around him.
In the vale of *Ceir*iog, 56
  that so loudly speaks,
"Fosterling of Death" was the
  lance, which slew his foes.
    Until I fall, in old age, 60
    into my dire, inevitable end,
    I shall take no pleasure,
    but in the praise of Urien. ᚦ

The Spoil of Taliesin & Praise of Urien.

MY BRAVERY emerges in time of stress : 1
  If wounded, shall I recover strength altogether ?
Verily, I saw, before any, the oppression, which I did not escape.
Every feather-brain made my message of no account. 4

62 Gweleis beu, pasc am leu ac am lys.　　　5
　Gweleis edn — dail o ðyfn a dowys.
21 Gweleis gaing, haval drain i blodeu.
　Neu·r weleis uð *hy·dreis* i ðeðveu.　　　8
　Gweleis *aeth* llyw gan draeth tra mäeu.
23 Bid wanar, nwy hachar gymyreu.
　Gwyrth vy nuð, mawr yn vuð i radeu.
25 Pen mäon milwyr *Mon* am·dereu.　　　12
　Preiff lwyvyð, rhein onwyð yw i arveu ;
26 Gwen i yscwyd, i rac-glyd, glas *i llenn* ;
63 Gloiw Hawd *Clyr*, glassav ður, vu i Urien :
2 *Neb* ni or·seiv i wyrth *glaiv*.　Gor·ðÿar　16
　gor Geriawg — *yn* llivawg, gor·lavar.
3 Gorian·re a or·ðwyre, a phob rhai
　sang ðilyv du veryð y·mordrei.
4 Uð, tra blawð, yn y glaw o·th ŵyð êl,　　20
　val ŷd melynawr yn neuað maer.
　Anheðawg, diffreidawg yn Aeron .
7 　Mawr i wŷn yn amwyn ac eillon ;
　Mawr ðyval, roði lâl am i alon.　　　24
　Gor·nerthed ysclyvied *gan* Vrython :
8 Mal rhod tân wy dreiglan dros elvyð ;
　Mal tonn *ant,* a·theithant Lwyvenyð ;
　Mal cyrchen cyv·liw Gwen a gweithen ;　　28
10 Val morÿawr ys mwynvawr yw Urien.
　Un i egin *ac* edlin go·driccawr.
　Un rhïeu a rhwyveu ði·raðiawr.
12 Un yw meirch mäon a mwth vilawr.　　32
　Ðechreu Mei, towyssei vyðinawr :
14 *Ev* ðenwy, ban ovwy, y werin.
　Eryr tir ! ys dy·hir, yth dremyn.
15 Aðunyð, y·ar orwyð ffysciolin,　　　36
　dyðyn ieil, werth yspeil, Daliessin.

I saw a land, with pastures round the clearing & the   5
  Court. I saw a bird, which brings leaves from the deep.
I saw a branch, like thorns its blossoms.
I saw a lord whose laws were *oppressive* :
I saw his *distress* along the shore beyond the plains.   9
Let him be a leader who will avoid the ravines.
A marvel is my lord ; great to us the benefit of his gifts.
The head of the chiefs of *Mona*'s men smites right & left.
Strong elm-*bows*, & ashen spears are his weapons ; his 13
  blue-covered shield, Gwen, was *ever* a shelter before him.
And flashing *Haute clere*, of bluest steel, had Urien.
None can withstand this wondrous glaive. The   16
  Ceiriog valley roars—in flood it thunders.
Great shouting rises, and everybody treads
  the honeycombed black swamps, in the great retreat.
The King, while fighting, disappears in the rain,   20
  like golden-yellow grain, into the steward's hall.
He sojourns, and shelters in Aeron :
Great his rage while defending with his aliens.
Strenuously he schemes to place Yale beyond his foes.
The ravaging by the Brythons was intensified :   25
Like a wheel of fire they revolve over the land ;
Like a wave they advance & traverse ILwyvenyδ.
As *they* press on the sight of Gwen means battle.
As a great prince greatly courteous is Urien.   29
His heir is the equal of the sojourner's etheling.
Chiefs are the same as rulers of low degree.
Great men's horses are as swift as beasts of chase.
Early in May he led armies :   33
He charms, when he visits, the people.
Eagle of the land ! far-reaching is thy glance.
Thou vowest, on thy lively steed, a culti-   36
  vated farm, a valuable spoil, to Taliesin.

63 Un yw gwrys gor ﬦawr prys a gor gwŷð.   38

17 Un brehyr *a* ffig*ur* pen arglwyð.

    Un yw hyð, a·r he*l*yð yn·i·vant.

    Un yw blaið banadl *wraið*, ac an·whant.

19 Un yw *rhad* a gwlad vad *'n* egin îr.   42

    Un weð sôn cadväon, a chedwyr.

    Un y drwg, ie*u*anc ðwg, a chenaw—

21 Nuð hael *vrad*, a herw wlad y·danaw.   45

    Ac os y dy·gwyð i ynni *rhag* Gwen.

22 ev gwnëid beirð *yn* byd yn ﬦawen.

    Cyn *elhwyv*, meirw vynhwyv veib Gwyðen.   48

24 Gwaladr *mad !* gwaeð gwenwlad *vo i* Urien.

ᚌ ᚌ ᚌ

Aðvwyn Geyryð.

Að·VWYN Gaer yssyð ar glawr gweilgi :
    Bid lawen Galan—eirian i rhi.

42 Ac yn amser*awr* mawr wrhydri,

20 ys gnawd gorun beirð uch með lestri.   4

    Dy·ðyvyð *Magnus* ar vrys iði—

22 dy·vrys i·r werlas, clas y ﬦichti.

    Ac a·m by*ch*, Dëws ! dros vyng·weði,

    pan gattwyf amod cymod a Thi.   8

24 Að·vwyn Gaer yssyð ar lydan lyn—

    dinas di·achor, mor o·i chylchyn :

26 Go·gyve*i*rch Brydein, cwð gyngein hynn :

    Blaen ﬦin ap Erbin, boed teu Vo*n* *r*ynn.   12

43 Bu goscorð—bu cerð yn eil mehyn ;

    ac eryr, uch wybr, a lwybr ranwyn.

3 Y·rag uð ffesig escar gychwyn :

    Clod wanar a wascar dy ym·ðuﬦyn.   16

Violence is the same in scrub and in forest.   38
A baron figures as a King.
The stag and the huntsman are alike in death.
The appearance of broom-root is a sign of great want.
Prosperity is the same as good land lush of growth.   42
The sound of battlefields and of warriors is alike.
The youth & the puppy are alike in mischief : *the youth*
  betrays a generous lord, & harasses his country.   45
And if his activity fail *before* 'Gwen',
  our country's bards would be made to rejoice.
Before I go, I wish dead the race of *Beauclerc.*   48
Beneficent Lord, the acclaim of a happy land be Urien's.

Þ Þ Þ

The Pleasant Strongholds.

PLEASANT the Kaer that looks down on the sea :   1
  Her year begins with feasting ; her chief is full of
  cheer.   And at times of valourous deeds, there is
  the usual to-do of the bards, over cups of mead.   4
Magnus suddenly descends upon her ; *then* hurries
  (back) to the green-blue (sea), the domain of the Picts.
Be Thou, O Lord, on the side of my prayer, when
  I am keeping the law of reconciliation to Thee.   8

Pleasant the Kaer on the broad water—an
  unapproachable stronghold, girt of the sea.
It faces Prydein, where it gives delight :
  Head of the line of Urien, thine be Mona's Rhynn.   12
There was a retinue & feast at another place, whose
  eagle, now above the sky, is traversing the milky way.
Against an adroit lord, put off an expedition :
  the repute of *such* a leader will scatter thy lines.   16

117

43 Aδ·vwyn Gaer yssyδ ar donn nawved : 17

5 Aδ·vwyn i gwerin, *rhvδ* i·n ym·wared :
Ni wnant eu *g*wynvyd trwy vevlhäed :

7 Nid ev eu devod bod yn galed. 20
Gau ni lavarav ar vyn·hrwyδed :—

8 Noc eiIIon Deudraeth gweII caeth Dyved.
Cyweithyδ, o rhyδ wleδ waredred,

10 gynnwys rhwng pob deu, *wr o·i g*iwed. 24

Aδ·vwyn ! Kaer yssyδ : a·i gwna·n gyman
meδud, a molud, ac avarn bann.

12 ILyvn i cherδeu *gwych*, yn i chalan,
am arglwyδ hywyδ, hëwr eiran. 28

14 Cyn *aeth* yn aδwyd, yn·erwin IIann,
a·m rhoes veδ a gwin o wydrin bann.

15 Aδ·vwyn Gaer yssyδ yn yr eglan :
Aδ·vwyn y rhoδir i bawb i ran. 32

17 Yn·Imbych adwen or·wen wylan—
cyweithyδ *hy*weδ veδei·r IIyssan.

18 Oeδ ev vyn *arver gael* nos Galan,
leδvdawd y·gan ri, rhyvel eiran, 36

20 a IIen ehöeg, a meδ *hweg* prain,
oni*d rh*wyδ tavawd ar *wawd* Prydein.

21 Aδ·vwyn Gaer yssyδ, a·i cyvrwy*δwn :*
oeδ meu y cer*δ*eu a δewiswn— 40

23 ni lavarav δaith, rhaith rhy·s·catwn.
Ni δ'ly gelenig ni wyppo hwn :—

24 Yscriven Brydein bryder brisiwn :
Yn yd wna tonneu eu hamgyffrwn, 44

26 perhëid hyδ·beII y geII dreiδwn.

Aδ·vwyn Gaer yssyδ yn Arδ*un*wein :
44 Go·chanwn i·m tud volud cowrein.

2 Aδ·vwyn ar i *t*hor, escor cyn·vrein : 48

Pleasant the Kaer above the ninth wave :   17
  Pleasant her people who bring us deliverance.
They do not find their happiness in making mis-
  chief, nor is it their custom to be hard-hearted.   20
I will not bear false witness on my tour—
  than Deudraeth's aliens, better the serfs of Dyved.
Her prince, an he give a feast of deliverance, will
  place, between every couple, one of his own people. 24

Pleasant the Kaer is : what make it perfect are
  mead-drinking, praising, & a high fee.
Harmonious, at her festival, the exquisite minstrelsy
  around her discerning lord, the cheerful dispenser. 28
Before he went to his destiny, in the oaken chest,
  he gave me mead & wine, from a high beaker.

Pleasant the Kaer in the haven :
  pleasant that all will receive their portion.   32
I know at Tenby a snow-white gull—the
  gentle lady of the soil, who ruled the little court.
It had been my lot to receive, on New Year's eve,
  a douceur from the lord of gleaming war ; and a 36
  green cloak ; & the luscious mead of the feast,
  till the tongue becomes fluent in Prydein's praise.

Pleasant the Kaer that I was wont to entertain :
  Mine were the poems, which I selected—   40
  I do not say it for effect I kept within my right.
He will deserve no New Year's gift, who knows not
  that Prydein's script will take care of *what* I prize :
As long as the waves maintain their motion,   44
  the parchment of the cell I occupied will endure.

Pleasant the Kaer in Arðunwent :
  I would sing to my country a skilful pæan, *for* 'tis
  pleasant on its Tor to renew old privilege.   48

44 Goδeg vrych dyɾviɾ—ys hir i hadein,
δy·chyrch var carreg—crec mor ednein.

4 ℓLid y·mywn tynghed, treiδ *o*ed tra maint :
A Bleiδ, uδ gor·ℓℓwyd, goreu affeint : 52

6 Dim ffynnei uch ℓℓad, pwyℓℓad coveint.
Bendith Culwyδ nev, a chydlev sein
a·n gwnel yn vrowŷr, gor·wŷr Owein.

8 Aδ·vwyn Gaer yssyδ ar lan ℓliant : 56
Aδ·vwyn yd roδir i bawb i whant.

10 Go·gyvarch Wyneδ : boed teu vwyant :
Gwaewawr cynrein, *Clar*, a δarvuant.

11 Verchyr gweleis wyr yng·hyvnovant ; 60
Ðyvieu bu er gwarth yδ ad·gorsant.

13 *O*d oeδ vriger coch, ac och ar dant,
y ℓluδed·g wyr—Gwyneδ aethant.

14 Am gevn ℓlech Vaelwy cylchwy vriwant : 64
Cwyδyn yng·H*w*m Ceɾŵyn ℓlu o garant.

卿 卿 卿

Marwnad Owein Gwyneδ . 1170.

(O)YD·WYV deryδ gwawd, a *lawd* vedyδ ;
dyd rw*y*δ*eu :* rhiv edeu eiδolyδ. 2

69 Cyv·rwng aℓℓ, ac *is*-aℓlt, ac echwyδ,
er·gryna Cuneδa greiseryδ.

12 Yng·Haer Veir a·cheriɾ lyw el*v*yδ : 5
Er rhynawd cyv·adawd gyv·ergyr :
an·whaneg — *dy·attreg* dân tra myr.

14 Ton *bron llew*—ℓluδiaw glew i gilyδ, 8
can cavas ym·hwel *gas* uch elvyδ.

15 *Darvu i hynt*, val uch gwynt wrth onwyδ :
Cyd·erchyn yng·hwm*plin* i gyvlyδ ;
a·chedwyn, a·chwelyn gerenhyδ. 12

120

The speckled, long-winged curlew, the sea-crake,   49
  chatters when disturbed, & flies to the top of a rock.
The malice in fate persists through endless time.
Lupus, the hoary bishop, effected deliverance : nothing
  prospers like the blessing & guiding of a monastery. 53
May the blessing of the dear God, & the united voice
  of the saints, make us countrymen of Owein's worthies.

Pleasant the Kaer on the tidal bank ;   56
  pleasantly is given to all their want.
Welcome Venedotia's *aid* : be thine the aggrandizement.
  The spearmen of the chieftain, *Clare*, have perished.
On Wednesday, I saw men on the march :   60
  On Thursday, to their shame, they had returned.
If the hair was gory, and sorrowful the harp, and
  men were aweary—to Gwyneð they went. Beyond
Maelwy's rocky ridge they ravage the surroundings :
  There fell in Cwm Cerwyn a host of friends.   65

絹 絹 絹

The Elegy of Owein Gwyneð.

I AM the lyrist of eulogy, who praises baptism,   1
  which confers graces : a host forsake their idols.
Twixt a high slope & a low, and the west,
  Cuneða's crosier-bearer is trembling.
In the citadel of Mary, the ruler of the land is loved. 5
  A little while since, he quitted for ever the field :
  Moreover, he is checking the rebellion over-seas.
The lion's heart is sick at the brave thwarting his
  fellow, for he met with a spiteful turn in his life. 9
His course ended, like the wind's moan in the ash trees :
  His clerics united at compline to pray for (his soul) ;
  (for) they treasured, they reciprocated his friendship. 12

69 *Ys cwynein,* veirδ cywrein ga*r* onwyδ :
   marw *vy n*av a gwynav *mor avar* :
19 Cwynitor—bu dewδor di·archar.   15
   Haval beis a dyvn-gleis, dy·chyffryn,
   am ym·adaw, tuδedaw *ad-δrychyn.*
21 *Ev noδei, meithrinei* galetlwm :
   *oe*δ luttach wrth *gonach* nac ascwrn.
22 Ys cyrria*d,* rhy·noδa*d,* cyn cu*δ*ie*d*   20
   a thydwed : i wyneb a gadwed.
23 *Bu* gan-waith, cyn bu laith, yn·orglwyd :
   Dy·chludent *i Arδunwent* ym·h*l*ym*n*wyd.
25 Go·gan*w*yd, rhag arswyd, i oer-*γ*erδed,
26 cyn bu daer δogn *amser* i duδed.   25
   Haid, haval am wyδwal cŵn *h*eb rwyd,
70 geinan *ve*δ—gwaeth Пyvreδ n*i* chavwyd.
2 Aδoed hun ni δimi*vn.* Achwynav,   28
   ac am lys, *ac* am grys Cuneδav.
3 Am ry·law haПt *wylaw,* hy·dre*u*la*v* :
   am vleiδ *trwn* a *g*arwn abaПav.
4 Gweδw veirδ *Mon*—a ogon, a ogav ;   32
5 a·r eil*on* amrywon a rivav.
   Rhy·ve*i*δawδ yn er·vlawδ, ac anav
6 can gorvy*n,* cyn cymun, Cuneδav.
   Rhy·n·ransei viw blith*i*on yr hav :   36
   Rhy·n·ransei eδystrawr, aeav :
8 Rhy·n·ransei win gloew, ac olew :
   Rhy·n·ransei dorv ceith rhag un crew.
10 Ev dyval *h*ogreП o gyff *g*lew :   40
   gwelad wr—pennadur bryd Пew.
11 ILuδ*i*ei veδei gy·wlad rhag *geu*—
   Mab Edern, tëyrn anaeleu !

122

The skilled bards bewailed the warrior, (but it is)   13
  the death of my lord that I lament so grievously.
He will be lamented—our stout, irresistible defence.
The shallow & deep pools are agitated alike, by the   16
  dying & covering of one their waters reflected.
He sheltered & fed the hard-faring folk ;
  but was more bare than a bone to the wastrel.
He was forgiven, and given sanctuary ere he was   20
  covered by the sod : his face was saved.
He was, ere his death, a hundred times in a litter :
  They bore him *to Arðunwent* into the conflict.   23
It was portended, from dread, that his ghost would walk
  abroad, ere the earth had, for any time, been his cover.
A crowd, like dogs around a lair un-netted, keeps watch
  on the grave : worse cowardice there never was.
  The sleep of destiny cannot be annulled.   28
I sigh for both the court and the cloak of Cuneða.
By reason of the flow of salt tears I am wasting away :
I pine for the brave countenance I loved. Like
  orphans are Mona's bards : whom they glorify I will ;
  and the harmonies they vary I shall esteem.   33
Cuneða ventured into dire conflict—into the scathe
  of a hundred combats, before his shriving. Among us
He would freely distribute milch cows in summer :   36
He would freely distribute war horses in winter :
He would freely distribute sparkling wine & oil :
He would freely distribute slaves against any stress :
He was a strenuous youth of a brave stock :   40
A man did he appear—a lord of lion aspect.
He would not allow a border prince to play false—
  the son of Edern was a tremendous ruler.

70 Dywal, di·archar, di·eding,   44
    am·ry·ffreu angheu dy·chyving.
    Ev go·borth i aes y*n* am*ðiffy*n :
14 Rhagorawl wyr gwrawl i unbyn.
    Dym·hun ! Cysc, vad gun tal being !
15 Cam dra, diva hun o goeling.   49

♪ ♪ ♪

𝔐arŵnaꝺ 𝔒ŵein.

Ɛ NEID Owein, *rhy·wyssid*,   1
  go·bwyꞁꞁid y ner o·i raid.
67 Rheged uð, a·i cuð tom clas ;
    Nid oeð vas i gy·wyðeid.   4
21 Isceꞁꞁ cerð a·i chlyd clodvawr ;
    Estiꞁꞁ gawr, a gwaew ꞁꞁiveid.
22 Can ni cheffir cystedlyð,
    i·n vyð ꞁꞁewenyð ꞁꞁadreid.   8
23 Medei alon Geveilawg ;
    Eisorawd i dad a·i daid.
24 Pan laðawð Owein ꞁꞁFlamðwyn,
    nid oeð vwy nog oeð gyv·reid.   12
25 Cyscid ꞁꞁLoegr lydan niver
    a ꞁꞁeuver yn eu ꞁꞁygeid.
    A·r rhai ni fföynt haeach,
68 oeð [hydra]ch, *ynvyttach haid :*   16
1 Owein a·i cospes yn ðrud,
    mal cnud yn dylud deveid.
2 Gwr gwiw, uch i amliw seirch,
    a roðei veirch i eircheid.   20
    Cyd a·s cronnei va*e*l caled
4 i·n rhanned : rhag*o*r i Eneid.

Bold, irresistible, irrepressible,   44
  he escapes from the jaws of death.
He supports his shield on the defensive :
Excellent men & brave were his chieftains.   47
Compose thyself ! Sleep, dear lord of the high bench !
It is wrong to disturb rest from a superstitious (dread).

⊽ ⊽ ⊽

The Elegy of Owein.

OHE Soul of Owein *has been summoned*,   1
  & his (spiritual) lord has come to his rescue.
A sanctuary's tomb now screens the lord
  of Rheged.   He was not low of ability, *but*   4
  the life-blood of poesy, & its illustrious shield :
Champion, *too*, of the javelin & flashing spear.
    That his equal is not to be found
      to us will be a secret joy.   8
He mowed down the enemies of Kyveilog :
  He was a fellow to his father & grandsire.
When Owein pressed the Flame-bearer hard,
  it was no more than was necessary.   12
A number of broad England's host sleep
  with the light still in their eyes :
But those who did not flee instantly
  were a rasher, foolisher crowd.   16
And Owein did punish them severely,
  as wolves punish sheep they pursue.
(Our) worthy hero, seated on gay trappings,
  presented horses to the begging fraternity.   20
Though he amassed riches, among us it
  was distributed ; his soul goes marching on.

125

Caer Sidi, a Chaer Ochren.

*G*OLYCHAF Wledig, pendefig ri,   1
    ledas i bennaeth dros draeth mundi.
54 Bu gyweir *gyvrang* yng·Haer Sidi,
19 drwy *or*·chestol hwyll a phryderi.   4
    Nu, neb cyn noc ev nid aeth iδi—
21 i'r g*er*wyn, dwvn *g*las cyvr*g*as gewri.
    Rhag preiδei Annwvn tost*l*ym gyni ;
    *h*yd vrawd parahawd inga*w*g weδi.   8
23 Tri Iloneid Prydwen yδ aeth iδi ;
    nam*yn* saith ni δyrreith o Gaer Sidi.

25 N*y*δwyv glod geinmyn : c*wyn* o·chlywid,
    yng·haer bedryvan p*an* δym·chwelid.   12
55 Yng·hy*w*eir oeδ pair pan ry·ver*w*id :
    O anadl naw morwyn go·chyneuid.
 2 Neu, Pair Pen Annwvn, pwy i *ff*ynud ?
    Gwrm*gant* am i oror, a mererid :   16
 4 Ni veirw vwyd *i* lwvr—*neu·s* rhy·dynghid :
    Deδv Ilw*y*th Ilë*en*awg δi·δaw δyrchid :
 5 Yn Ilaw Ilemen*i*g yδ edewid :
    a rhag porth uffern Ilugyrn loscid.   20
 7 A phan aeth Arthur drafferth lechlyd,
    namyn saith ni δyrreith o gaer veδid.

 9 N*y*δwyv glod geinmyn : c*wyn* glywator
    yng·haer bedryvan—ynys bybr-δor.   24
10 Uch*er* am i huch*der* gymyscetor :
    Gwin gloew y gwirawd rhag i gorδgor :
12 Tri Iloneid Prydwen yδ aeth ar vor ;
    namyn saith ni δyrreith o gaer rigol.   28

King Richard at Joppa & Acre. 1197.

I WILL praise the King, the noble chief, who   1
  spread his supremacy over the world's strand.
Complete was his victory at Whirlpools Fort,
  by reason of extraordinary thought & care.   4
Now, no one before him entered this vortex,
  this deep *close* of fearsome giants.
Poignant the affliction caused by the herds of the
  Abyss : till doom will last the cry of distress.   8
Thrice filled Prydwen sailed thereto :
  Only seven returned from Whirlpools Fort.

May I spin fine praise : moaning was heard
  in the quadrangular fort, when it was overthrown.   12
Attuned was the cauldron after much boiling ;
  By the breath of the Nine Muses the fire was kindled.
This Cauldron of the Head of the Abyss, what is it like ?
  It has a dusky band around the edge, set with pearl : 16
  It will not cook a coward's food—him it has forsworn :
  The Code of the literary tribe out of it arose—
In the keeping of the minstrels it was left.
  Before Inferno's portal (its) lamps were burning.   20
And when Arthur went into the rocky toils,
  only seven returned from the fortress taken.

May I spin fine praise : moaning was heard in the
  quadrangular fort—the tor with the boisterous gate.
Its top with the twilight was confused :
  Sparkling wine was the liquor set before its council :
Thrice full did Prydwen sail the sea :
  only seven returned from the citadel of the frith.   28

127

55 Ni o·bryn *ev* ffavr Πwʋr lywiadur :   29
    Tra Chaer Wydr gwelsid wrhyd Arthur.

15 Tri ugein canhwr a seiv y·ar mur—
    an·hawδ ynɪ·aδrawδ a·i gwyliadur.   32

17 Tri Πoneid Prydwen aeth gan Arthur ;
    namyn saith ni δyreith o gaer o·vur.

19 Ni obryn *ev* ffavr Πwʋr yng·hylchwy :
    Ni wδant py *bryd* perhid δypwy—   36

20 Py awr ym·*hylgein* y ganed twy—
    Pwy ry·wnaeth arnynt aeth dol *Gan*dwy.

22 Ni weδant vras ych brych y pen rwy(f)—
    saith ugein cygwng yn i aerwy.   40

24 A phan aeth Arthur avrδwl ovwy ;
    namyn saith ni δyrreith o gaer *G*andwy.

25 Ni o·bryn *ev* ffavr Πwʋr eu gohen :
    Ni wδant py *bryd* perid dy·ben—   44

56 Py awr ym·*hylgein* ganed perchen—

2 Pwy wŷl a gadwant ariant ym·hen.
    A phan aeth Arthur avrδwl gynhen,

3 namyn saith ni δyrreith o gaer Ochren.   48

    Myneich δy·chwynyn val un yng·hor,

5 o gyvranc uδyδ a·r Gwiδanhor.
    A·i un hynt *pob* gwynt ? un dwr *pob* mor ?

7 A·i un Πev *torv* a thwrv di-achor ?   52

    Myneich δy·chw*y*nynt *am hynt* veiδawl,

8 o gyvranc uδyδ a·r Gwiδanhawr.
    Ni wδant yscein deweint a gwawr ;   55

10 neu wynt, pwy i hynt—pwy i rynnawr ?
    Py va ry·δiva, py dir aplawr.

11 Boed se*i*nt yn·i·vant *weinant* aΠawr.
    Golychav Wledig, pendevig mawr.   59

15 *Bid i·m* na bwyv drist : Crist a·m gwaδawl.

He will not curry favour of the cowardly governor : 29
Beyond Glass-town was seen Arthur's heroism.
Three score centuries stand upon the wall—
It is not easy to converse with the sentinel. 32
Thrice full Prydwen went with Arthur :
  only seven returned from the walled town.

He will not curry favour of the slack on their round :
They know not when will happen what is coming—
  at what hour of morning the check began ; *nor* 37
  who wrought their sorrow on the plain of Candevia.
They will not yoke *Saladin's* brindled, giant ox
  which has seven score knots in its tie. 40
And when Arthur went on his sad expedition,
  only seven returned from Candevia.

He will not curry favour of the slack in command :
  They do not know when happened the end— 44
  at what hour of morning the victory was won.
Who will detect secreters of treasure in the mouth ?
And when Arthur went into the sad struggle,
  only seven returned from " Ochren" fort. 48

The monks wailed like one man in unison, because
  of the adventure of the king with the Viedenese.
Holds every wind to one course ? Is every sea one water ?
Is the shout of a crowd the same as irrepressible thunder?

The monks wailed because of the daring journey— 53
  the adventure of the King with the Viedenese.
They do not know that night-watch extends to dawn,
  nor the course of the wind, nor what its impulses— 56
  what spot it devastates, what land is buffeted.
May the servers of the altar be saints after death.
  I will praise the King, the great nobleman.
  May I not be sad : Christ be my heritage. 60

Marwnad Richard . 1199.

* * * * * * *

51 *Amser* croes *grwydriad, ban* wys*iad* byd, 1
   bu deu dêg ar wlad wledychyssid :
2 *Un* haelhav, berthav o·r ry·aned—
   Un terwyn wenwyn, gwae y giwed :   4
4 Ev dorres ardal deir gwaith yng·had,
   ac ni vyδ cor-wŷδ i wŷr i dad.
5 *Y llall, mal* puvawr a·theghwys *wlad.*
   Syrth, yng·o·δiwaw Alexander,   8
7 yn hual eurin : Gwae ! carcharer :
   Ni pheII garcharwyd—i angheu δyvu
8 ar le y cavas ergyr o lu.
   Neb, *er oed, gwell* ni *roed yn*·aerawd :   12
   Meueδ beδ, berthrwyδ o·r aδwyndawd.
   [Haer Alexander gymerth yna :—
   Ynys Sur—*dinas* yng·wlad Syria—
11 A·r wlad δinistrad *tra* din te*rr*a—   16
13 Ciwdawd Babilon, a *llys* Susa—
12 Gwlad Persia, Media, Yk*bat*anna—
13 Yni*a*leδ Parthia a, parth India,
   Mawr Wlad Galdaria, bychan i da,   20
15 hyd yr ymδug tir—tywarch yna.
   Yd wnahont eu bryd wrth eu her*w*a :
   Cyweδant wystlon i Europa :
17 An·rheithant wladoeδ, wysioeδ terra :   24
   Gwychr gwerynt wrageδ, gor·*v*ynt yna—
19 Bron-loscent y·gan wyleδ gwastad,
   a godei avar ban adroδ*a*d.   27
20 A δy·go*ll*ynt vraint gwneint ben brithred :
21 Milwyr vagent δawn ban attoded.

The Elegy of King Richard.

*   *   *   *   *   *   *

At the time of the Crusade when the world was   1
summoned, two fair ones ruled *our* land :
The one most generous, & sweetest of those born.
The other irascible ; woe to the state :   4
  He burst our border three times in war, *but*
  he never will be a covert to his father's men.
The former like an apple-tree beautified the land :
While overcoming Alexander, he falls into   8
  the golden fetter.   Alas, he was imprisoned, but
  not for long.   His death came on the spot
  where he received the arrow from the host.
None better was ever interred : the   12
  passport of the grave is the beauty of holiness.
[Irresistible Alexander had taken
  the *island citadel* of Tyre in Syria, which he
  over-ran *beyond* the earthen ramparts (of Gaza)—
  the state of Babilon, & *the palace* of Susa—   17
  the countries of Persia, Media, Ecbatana—
  the Parthian desert and, towards India,
  the Great Hot Country (of little good),   20
  as far as the land went—morass beyond.
They do as they please on their wanderings :
They despatch hostages to Europe : They   23
  plunder the countries of the nations of the earth ;
They ruthlessly tamed, then violated the women,
  whose breasts burnt with constant humiliation,
  which gave rise to fresh sorrow when it was told. 26
Those who lost their freedom raised the whirlwind :
The soldiers received a boon by marrying.

51 Rhïaḷḷu a vu varw y·rac syched—   30
   eu gau gowiḷḷeu, ac eu miled :
23 A·s gwenwynwys gwres cyn no·u trevred.]
24 Nev wlad i·th weison pan ðiffoðed :
   Ni byð i·th escar escor ḷḷuðed,   34
25 rhag goval yr hual a·i agaled.
   Cyn no hyn *han*ffei gweḷḷ ðigoned
52 i·m harglwyð ḷḷad ḷḷwyð gwlad gogoned—
   un oror oreu Jor ystlyned.   38
2 Diwyccwyv ! Wnelhwyv, genhyv gyv·red—
   A·r sawl a·m clywho boed meu ý huned.
4 Digonwynt voð Duw cyn gwasc tydwed. 41

❀ ❀ ❀

Echrys Ynys.

ECHRYS ynys,   1
   gwawd huðianus—
68   gwrŷs go·betror.

   Mon vad, gogei ;   4
7 gwrhyd ervei,
   y·Menei ðor.

   Lleweis wirawd—   7
8 gwin a bragawd,
   gan vrawd escor.

   Tëyrn orwyv :   10
9 diweð pob rhwyv,
   rhewinetor.

   Tristlawn deon   13
10 yr archadon,
   can rhychitor :

132

A hundred thousand died from thirst,
  with their false brides, & their beasts : the   31
  heat destroyed them before their return home.]
The heavenly kingdom be thy men's heritage at death ;
Thine enemies will never shake off their weariness,
  because of the care of the fetter, & the hardship (thereof).
Or ever this happened better was prepared   36
  for my lord, the blessings of the Land of Glory—
  the unparalleled clime associated with God.
May I amend ! what I do keeps step with me.
Mine be the prayer of all who hear me : Let them   40
  do the will of God ere the pressure of the sod.

卐   卐   卐

The Island Dread, 1197.

THE island dread   1
  has muffled the muse—
    upheaval everywhere.

It shook bonnie Mon ;   4
  Bravery triumphed,
    at Menei's door.

I drank liquor—   7
  wine and bragget,
    with an uterine brother.

The prince I will vanquish :
  The end of every ruler   11
    is to be ruined.

Very sad the chieftains
  of the over-lord,   14
    because he is buried.

133

68 Nid vu, nid vi,   16
11 yng·hymelri,
     i gyv·eisor.

     Pan ẟoeth adon,   19
12 o wlad Wydion—
     Seon dewẟor,

     Gwenwyn py·r ẟoeth ;   22
13 peẟei beunoeth,
     meinẏoeth dymhor.

     Cwyẟynt gyvoed,   25
14 ni bu glyd coed—
     gwynt yng·oror.

     Math yr eurgryẟ,   28
15 hudwyth gelvyẟ,
     rhy·ẟelwei vor.

     Ym·yw Gwydion,   31
16 ae vamaeth, Don,
     yẟ oeẟ gynghor.

     Twyll-dâl roẟawd   34
17 ffyrv ffodïawg—
     ffyrv ẟi·achor.

18 Cadarn gyngres   37
     i varanres,
     ni bu warth-vor.

19 Ilawen gyveẟ,   40
     ym·hob gorseẟ,
     wnelid i bor.

20 Cun Tynaethwy,   43
     hyd tra vwyv vyw,
     Crybwylletor.

There never was, nor will   16
  be, in time of trial,
    his equal.

When the chief came   19
  from Gwydion's country—
    the stout defence of Seon,

The Plague also came —   22
  it stalked nightly, through
    a lovely summer :

Contemporaries fell ;   25
  The woods were no shelter
    from the tempest in the land.

Math, the golden cordwainer—
  the expeditious craftsman,
    bephantomed the sea.   30

In the time of Gwydion,
  & of his foster-mother, Don,
    there was a *modus operandi*.

He gives to illusive payment
  a fortunate appearance—   35
    an irresistible semblance.

The mighty muster,   37
  of his battle array,
    had never been to sea.

Joyous feasts were made,   40
  at every station,
    for the chief.

The lord of Dinoethwy
  while I live, shall   44
    be commemorated.

68 Am bwy gan Grist,   46
    hyd na bwyv drist,
      ran ebostol.

22 Hael archadon,   49
    gan engylion,
      cynwysetor.

11.

ECHRYS Ynys   52
    gwawd huði*a*nis—
      gwrys go·chyva :

24 Rhag bug*eil*-was,   55
    Cymry ðivas,
      aros ara.

25 Dragonawl ben—   58
    (Priodawl berchen
      ym·Retonia),
26 ðiva r Gwledig,   61
    or·bendevig,
      a·i ða derra.

69 *Y* teir morwyn,   64
    wedy *di*rwyn,
      ðygnant eu tra :

2 Er·ðygnant wir,   67
    ar vor a thir—
      hir eu trestra.

    Wy wir honyn,   70
3   na ðigonyn
      ðim go·ðrutta.

    Ceryðus wyv,   73
4   na chrybwyllwyv,
      a·m rhy·wnel ða.

May I have with Christ,   46
that I may not be sad,
   The portion of an apostle.

The bounteous over-lord,
 by the angels, has been
   encompassed.   51

II.

T HE island dread   52
  has muffled the muse —
 Upheaval is general

Against the regent, who   55
 has devastated Kymry,
  enduring patiently.

The military head —   58
 (the rightful owner
  being in Bretonia),
 is eating up the King —   61
  an august nobleman,
   and his good land.

The three maidens,   64
 after the winding,
  toil at their task.

They do truly, toil hard   67
 on sea & land : long
  their arduous labour.

They truly asserted,   70
 that they did
  nothing at all rash.

I am to blame   73
 for not mentioning
  one who benefits me :

69 I lary lywy,   76
     pwy gwaharδwy?—
  5   pwy attrevna?

   Y llary adon   79
   a gynheil Mon,
  6   mywn go·wala.

   A·m bwy gan Grist,   82
   (hyd na bwyv drist
  7   o δrwg, o d*r*a),
   ran trugareδ,   85
   i wlad Rhieδ—
  8   bucheδ gyva.   ⱶ

Crogiad Madawg vab Maelgwn.

MADAWG mur menwyd   1
     a grogid cyn beδ :
66 Bu was en·rhyveδ
     o gamp a chyveδ—   4
 11 Ma*d*-wychr cyn lleas ;
     i·w lawr dy·m·wystlas.
 12 Bu Erov greulawn :
     llewenyδ n*i* chawn :   8
 13 Tristid anwogawn,
     a or*eu* 'r Creulawn.
   Am vradu Jessu,
 14   ac ev yn credu,   12
   mae Cred yn gwgu—
   daear yn crynu—
   elvyδ yn gar*m*u—
 15   cysteg, ac ar*s*wyd,   16
   *a*m vedyδ ar gr*w*yd*r*.

138

His liberal provision—   76
who shall check?—
who control?

(He is) the liberal lord,   79
who maintains Mon,
in abundance.

May I have with Christ—   72
(that I may not be sad,
because of evil & excess),
the portion of mercy   85
for the Lord's country—
a perfect life.   ⸕

King John hangs Madawg . 1212.

ⓂADAWG the bulwark of genius   1
was hanged, or (he came to) the
grave.   He was a wonderful youth
in feats of skill & entertainment :   4
Good & brave, or he was slain, he gave
himself a hostage for his country.
But " Herod " was blood-thirsty ;
& we shall, no more, have joy :   8
Overwhelming sorrow
the Cruel One wrought.
For betraying Jesus,
and he a believer,   12
Christendom is wrath—
the earth is quaking, &
the elements are howling :
(There is) affliction & horror   16
because baptism is missing.

139

66 *Dryg*lam anwogawn
16 a oryw 'r Creulawn,
   yn myned, yn y drevn,   20
17 ym·hlith oer gethern,
   yng·waelawd uffern.   ᚦ

ꟿartꞩawꞩ Dylan · · 1212.

ꓑN Duw uchav,   1
   Dewin doethav,
67   mwyhav amner.
10 Pwy·*n* dylivas ;   4
   Pwy a·*n* swynas,
   a *gras* trahael.
11 Neu, gynt nog Ev,
   pwy vu dangnev   8
   ar reꞩv go·vel ?
12 Gwrthriv ga*n* dra*eth*,
   Gwenwyn a wnaeth—   12
13   gwaith gwythloneꞩ.
   Gwan*as* Dylan —
   adwythig *v*an,
14   dreis yn hydr-weꞩ.   16
   Ton Iwerꞩon,
   a thon Vanaw,
15   a thon Ogleꞩ :
   a thon Prydein—   20
   torv oeꞩ virein
   ym·heir*anne*ꞩ.
16 Golychav Dad,
   Duw, dovyꞩad   24
   gwlad, heb omeꞩ :
17 Creawdr celi
   a·n cynnwys ni,
   yn·hrugareꞩ.   28

Overwhelming the fate that will
overtake the cruel one, when
he goes, in the order of things,
among the heartless fiends
into deepest hell.

The harrying of Dylan (point).

THE One God supreme,
the wisest prophet, (&)
the greatest almoner :
Who threaded our warp ;
Who blessed us with
grace abounding.
Now, who, before His time,
acted as harmony
on the spirit of war ?
The hostile force along the
coast raised discontent—
it rouses evil passions.
The Point of Dylan—
a miserable place, the
force pillages ruthlessly, i.e.
the crew from Ireland,
and the crew from Man,
& the crew from Gogleð,
and the crew from the 'South'—
a company which excelled
in feats of engineering.
I worship the Father,
God, the indisputable
Ruler of the land.
The Creator of heaven
will encompass us about
with mercy.

(𝔊𝔴𝔯)𝔥𝔞𝔡 𝔈𝔯𝔬𝔟 . 1213.

Y̶M·CHWELES elvyẟ,   1
  val *troi* nos yn ẟyẟ.
65 Go·ẟyvod clodryẟ—
   Erov beir vedyẟ.   4
   Ev a ẟywedei,
66   angheu na·s rhivei.
   Y·mordei, *i* yscwyd
   arnaw a dorr*id*.   8
 2 Erov, sywessid,
   "ermi*d* Loegr i gyd."
 3 Pedeir *llorv* cyhyd,
   rhuẟeur ar eu hyd—   12
   Colovneu Ercwl
 4 ni·s ar·vei*l* bygwl.
   Bygwl, ni·s beiẟei ;
 5 g*w*res heul, ni·s gadei.   16
   Nid aeth neb i·*r* nev,
   hyd i *warog*aeth ev.
 6 Erov, m*il* ffossawd,
   ban am·duẟ tywawd,   20
 7 A·s rhoẟwy Trindawd
   drugareẟ ẟyẟbrawd—
 8   wyndawd heb eiseu. ⅌

𝔐𝔞𝔯(𝔱𝔥)𝔞𝔴𝔡 𝔈𝔬𝔯𝔯𝔬𝔦 𝔪𝔞𝔟 𝔇𝔞𝔶𝔯𝔶.

D̶YFFYNHAWN lydan ẟy·leinw aches :
  i ẟaw a·i hepcyr—di·bris i bres.   2
66 Mar(th)awd Corroï a·m cyffröes.

20   Over dovi gwr garw i an·wydeu,
   a oeẟ vawr i ẟrwg—mwy ni·s cigleu. 5
22   Mab Dayry ẟalei arwr Deheu ;
   dathlawg oeẟ i glod cyn no·i adneu.

142

John submits (to the Pope).

HIS reversal of polity is   1
 like *turning* night into day.
It is a glorious event—
 Herod brings about baptism.   4
He was wont to boast
 that he would not heed death.
On the coast his shield
 was shivered upon his arm.   8
Herod, it was prophesied, would be
 in conflict with all England.
Four pillars of equal length,
 all covered with ruddy gold—   12
the pillars of Hercules,
 no rebellion will bring down.
He did not dare the interdict : he 15
 would not quit the sun's warmth.
No one went to heaven
 until his submission.
Herod, of conflicts innumerable, 19
 when the sand shall cover,
May the Trinity grant him
 mercy, on the day of doom,
  & complete felicity. ⊢   23

The Smashing of King John . 1215.

THE spreading flood fills the road-stead ; His 1
 son-in-law thrusts him aside & recks not his
adversity. The smashing of Corroï has moved me.

Vain is the appeasing of a man of harsh passions,
 who did much evil—I never heard of greater. 5
This son of Dairi detained the hero of the South,
 who was renowned before his imprisonment.

143

66 Dyffynhawn lydan ðy-leinw nanneu :   8
    i ðaw a·i hepcyr — dy·vrys Ðeheu.

25   Marᵗhawd Corroï genhiv inheu·
    Over dovi &c.

26 Dyffynhawn lydan ðy·leinw y Ꝇyr :   12
67 Rhysaeth ðy·chyrch draeth di·wng ebyr.
    Gwr a werescyn *gylchyn Deheu* ;

2   M[a]wr i varanres *torres gaereu.*
    Ac wedi mynaw, myned trevyð :   16

3   a[eth]ant wy vrodyr vre Wynionyð.

    Tra mi 'm·Uðugre, vore, dugawr
    chweðleu am gwyð*aw* awyr hyd lawr.

5   Cyvre*ing* Corroï a Chocholyn —   20
    Ꝇiaws eu tervysc am eu tervyn.

6   Tarðei·*n* pen *i* amwyn gwerin aðvwyn.

    Caer yssy i Gulwyð, ni gwyð, ni grŷn :
8   Gwyn vyd yr eneid a·i harobryn.   24

❦ ❦ ❦

Marwnaꝺ uthyr Ben.

MYVI vu*m* *v*oꝇtawd yn·hrydar ;   1
    ni pheidwn, rhag Ꝇu heb wyar.

71 Myvi a elwit Gor·lassar :
9   'ng·wre*g*ys, bu envys i·m hescar.   4

    Myvi, tywyssawg yn·hyweꝇ :
    a·m rhithwy*s* a·m dug yng·haweꝇ.

11 Myvi, eil *S*awyl yn Arðu,
    ni pheidwn heb wyar rhag Ꝇu.   8
    Myvi a amug, wrth vessur,
13 yn·i·vant, a·charant Gasnur.

    Neu·r or·ðyvneis waed am Wythur —
15 cleðyval hydr rhag meib Cawrnur.   12

The spreading flood fills the channels : his son- 8
  in-law thrusts him aside and hastens South.
Of the smashing of Corroi will I sing.
    Vain is the appeasing, &c.

The spreading flood fills the tidal reaches : an 12
  expedition seeks the strand of spacious Abers.
Our hero over-runs the ambit of the South
  with a great host : he broke its Castles.
After penetrating (everywhere) all turn homeward :
  The brothers went to the height of Gwynionyð. 17

While I was at Buðugre, one morning, news
  was brought of the skies falling down.
"John" struggles with "Ꝉlewelyn"— 20
  many their quarrels over their frontier.
Our prince arose to defend the honest poor.

The loving God's citadel will neither fall,
  nor totter.   Blessed the soul that shall win it. 24

      ❦   ❦   ❦

The threnody of uthyr Ben.

I WAS a bolt in the tumult : 1
    I would shed blood to stop a host.

  I was called Blue Enamel's Glory ; my
    girdle was as a rainbow to my enemy. 4

  I was a prince in disguise : He, who
    enchanted me, placed me in the creel.

  I was the fosterling of *S*awyl in Arðu :
    I would shed blood to stop a host. 8
  I defended, in reason, the friends of
    Casnur on (his) evanishment.

  I drew blood to avenge Gwythur— 11
    Daring the fight against the sons of Cawrnur.

K   145

71 Myvi a *geveis*, wrth vessur,   13
  nawved rhan yng·wrhyd Arthur.

16 Myvi a dorreis gant caer :
    Myvi a leδeis gant maer.   16

18 Myvi a roδeis gant Ꝉen :
    Myvi a leδeis gant pen.

19 Myvi a roδeis, i Henben,
    gleδyvawd gor·vawr gynghaꝉen.   20

20 Myvi *a d*ereu daran hyδ,
    he*l*yator i deith pen mynyδ.

22 Gweδw, i·m cov, Hyδwn o gilyδ :
    Nid oeδ vyd, ni bei eisiꝉyδ.   24

23 Mi·d·wyv varδ moladwy, cywreint,
    a gân *am* vraenad eryr gwytheint :

25 Avagδu a·i deubu yng·Him *n*eint,   27
    ban ym*s*yrth bydr*ŵ*yd rhwng dwy gainc.
    Dringaw i nev (oeδ ev vy chwant),
72 a·r eryr, rhag ovn am·heirant.

  2 Wyv barδ a thelynawr—
     wyv pibyδ a chrythawr   32
  3 i seith ugein cerδawr
     δy·or·vawr gynghaꝉen—
  4 Bu *g*ethlyδ ry·vreinad ;
     hu, escu*d*, δa*t*ceinad.   36

    I vab δy·veirw nad—
  5 δy·veirw δewindab,
     ar vlaen vyn·havawd,
     i draethu mar*th*awd.   40

    Handid, o·m main *g*ani*a*d,
  7 gwrthgloδiad w*ŷ*d Prydein,
     hüyscein ym·hwyꝉad.

  8 Wledig Nev ! *Clyw* 'ng·hennad,
     na·m *gomeδ dy* döad.   45

I obtained, by measure,   13
the ninth part of Arthur's prowess.

  I destroyed a hundred forts :
  I killed a hundred castellans :   16
  I bestowed a hundred tents :
  I cut off a hundred heads :

I administered, to Henben,
the stroke of the great enchanter.   20
I enchanted a fair-sized stag,
that was driven to the mountain top.
Desolate, I remember, was Hyδwn without a 24
partner : it was not life without an offspring.
I am a skilled bard, worthy of praise, who
sings of the putrefying of the chafing Eagle.
Avagδu came to him in the dales of Cim, when 27
his putrid flesh was falling between the branches.
To climb with the Eagle to heaven, for fear
of dissolution — that was my desire.

  I am bard and harpist —
  I am piper and crowder ;   32
    to seven score minstrels
    of the very great enchanter,
    who had been a highly gifted singer,
    and a spirited, fluent, reciter.   36

  His son will inspire the dirge,
  and prepare the witchery,
  on the tip of my tongue,
  to tell of the death.   40

  Mayhap, by my trifling song, the
  wrath of Prydein has been soothed,
  dispersing itself into wisdom.

  Ruler of Heaven, give ear to my embassy:
  Do not deny me thy roof-tree.   45

Cᴀɪɴ gyveδwch   1
   y·am dawelwch—
72 elwch amhad.

10 Peryδ ang·hawr,   4
   roed yn elawr,
   rhy·yscrinad.

11 Milein ffo Caw—
   Llynghes rhagδaw—   8
   mwyedig vrad.
   Draig ym·vryssiei,

12 oδuch Ⲓyreu,
   yn Ⲓestreu Ⲓad.   12
   Ⲓad yr eur-daw,

13 meδ-gorn yn Ⲓaw,
   Ⲓawr yscïad.

14 Y·modrydav,   16
   ev ry·th·iolav,
   yn rhïyδ mad.
   Buδugawl Veli !
   am·Hanogan ri ;   20

15 rhy·geidw yn teithi.
   Ynys vei Veli—
   teithawg vyδ iδi :

16 Pym pennaeth δybi,   24
   o Wyδyl Ⲓichti—

17 o berth gadeithi—
   o geneδl ysci.
   Pymp ereiⲒ δybi,   28

18 o *Ffreinc* Normandi.
   Wheched, rhyveδ ri,

19 o hau hyd vedi.
   Seithved, o heni,   32
   dym·werid dros li.

20 Wythved, Linx a vi—
   ni·d Ⲓwyδ *i* escori.   35

148

PLEASANT the festivity—   1
   a thank offering for peace—
   the rejoicing of many races.
The unprincely sovereign,   4
   who was placed in a litter,
   has been entombed.
Sullen the flight of " John,''
   fronting him a fleet, and   8
   ever-growing treason.
The " Dauphin " hastened,
   up the tidal reaches,
   in goodly vessels.   12
The glorious son-in-law,
   mead-horn in hand, blesses
   the country's deliverance.
At the mother-court   16
   I will greatly praise thee,
   our beneficent prince.
Victorious " Llywelyn ",
   son of the chief Manogan,   20
   will maintain our privileges.
The island that was Beli's,
   will know wandering (spirits) :
Five chiefs will come   24
   of the Irish Picts—
   of fine fighting mettle—
   of a ravaging race.
Five others will come—   28
   the *Franks* of Normandy.
A sixth, a wonderful King
   from seeding time to harvest.
A seventh, outside *the island*,   32
   will be delivered over-sea.
An eighth, a Lynx will be—
   his birth will bring no blessing.

DAROGANEU.

DYS·GO·GAN Awen *Ffreinc* δy·vryssyn—
    maranheδ a meueδ hêd genhyn :
70 A phennaeth ehalaeth IFra*w* unbyn,
    wedy heδ, δy·anheδ bob mehyn. 4
22 Gwlad veirw—dy·*chyrchir Mon*—
    tyrvhit hyd Valäon.
  23 Ymδeithig i haelon—
    ILuδedig *marchogion*— 8
  24 Gwlat, gwehyn bargodion.

    Coĺawd gymyrreδ
  25   yn rhy·gystlyneδ
      o bennaeth weison. 12

  26 Rhy·δybyδ ILeinawg,
    a vyδ gwr hwannawg
  71   i werescyn Mon.

    A rhewin Wyneδ— 16
  2 i heithav, a·i pherveδ,
    a chymmer wystlon.

  4 Dy·δaw gwr o guδ,
    a wna gyvamruδ 20
    a chad yng·hyn·don.

  3 Ys dig i wyneb ;
    ni·d estwng i neb, 23
    na *Ffreinc* na Saeson.

  5 Araĺ a δyvyδ—
    peĺenawg lywyδ,
    ĺewenyδ Brython. 27

PROGNOSTICATIONS.

THE Muse prophesies that the *French* will hie away—
 that their people & possessions will fly with them—
that the wide supremacy of the *Aber*ffro princes,
when peace is made, will settle everywhere.   4
    The land will seethe—*Mon will be attacked*—
upheaval will extend as far as Balaon.
Our princes will be wanderers—
Our knights will be worn out : & men   8
of the border will exhaust our land.

    Kymry will lose its status
    from too much intercourse
      on the part of her princes.   12

    There will come to Ꝇeinog
    a man who will be eager
    to conquer Mon :

    He will ruin Gwyneδ—   16
    its extremity, & centre,
    & will take hostages.

    A hero will come out of the void,
    who will execute bloody work,   20
    & give battle in the breakers.

    Fierce of aspect
    he will cringe to no one—
    nor *French*, nor Saxon.   24

    Another will come—
    a wandering chieftain,
    the joy of the Brython.   27

Canu Owein ap Kadwgan.

RHY·δyrchavwy Duw, ar blwyv Brython,
  arwyδ Ꝉewenyδ—Ꝉüyδ o Von.
72 Cyv·rysseδ Gwyneδ, brys or·chorδion.

25 IFaw claer o bob aer caffael gwystlon :   4
    Dybyδant fföwys yn·ẇys ffyꝉon :
73 Gwyr gor·wyn, gôrynt ar eu deδvon.

    Deu *gun* lüyδant, byδant gysson,
2 yn un reδv, un eir, gyweir, gymon :   8
    cyv·ranant yn iawn, *cyv*iawn väon.

4 Ban welych wr*th*ryn am Lyn Aeron—
    Ban vo trwm Towi, a Theivi·n Ꝉon,
    wy wnant aer, ar vrys, am lys Lonion.   12

6 Y gau ni·s dewis, yn os·*cor*δion,
    ni nothwy δinas rhag *tras* wythlon.

7 Dyn clud, dyn maerud, dyn dar·ymson—
    neu·d oeδ lwyr δengyn—dyn rhïeδon.   16

9   Ban δyvu Gadwgawn
      dros eigawn lwerδon
    yδ atrevnwys neδ yr arδ Verion :
    Ni bu hir yno heb ovalon :   20
11 *Ys* moch y clywis *am* geisadon—
    am varchawg mor daer am gaer Lonion—
12 am δïal Ithel ar an·wynion—
    am ware peꝉe*n* a phen Saeson.   24

13 Ys tra·bluδ Cath Vraith ang·hyvreithlon :
    O Ryd ar Daradr hyd Wygyr Von,
15 Jeuanc δi·vwynas δinas mäon.

    O·r pan amlygir mel y·meiꝉon   28
17 gadent ý hamrydar, a·u hamrysson :
    ni·d di·wystl godi dig wrth alon.

To Owein ap Cadwgan.

MAY God hoist on high, over the Brython race, the 1
  flag of rejoicing : the armed host is leaving Mon :
The strife in Gwyneδ speeds away the great retinues.

Great the glory of receiving hostages, after every fight :   4
  Those that fled into the dense thicket are returning ;
  and the hoary elders are brooding over the laws.

Two *princes* are marshalling—they will act harmonious-
ly, with one impulse, in accord, equipped, & orderly :   8
they will divide fairly and equitably their territories.

When you see trouble beyond the Vale of Aeron—
  when the Towy is sad, and the Teivi is feasting,
  they will hurriedly lay siege round Lonion's Court.   12

The traitor will not choose for his champions, those who
  will not hold the fort against the outraged kindred.

The abductor, a steward's kin, a notorious fellow,
  was a thorough villain of patrician descent.   16

      When Cadwgan returned
        over the Irish sea,
He set in order a nook in hilly Merion :
He was not long there free from cares :   20
He soon heard about men seeking him—
  about the Knight so ardent around Lonion fort—
  about the vengeance of Ithel on the recreants—
  about the rolling in play of Saxon heads.   24

Troubled is the striped Cat of the foreigners : from
  Taradr Ford (on the Wye) to Kemeis bay in Mon,
  Owein afflicted the strongholds of the territorial lords.

From the time honey is produced in clover,   28
  they quitted their tumult and their conflict :
To stir a foe's ire is to give hostage (to fortune).

Canu Cadwgan aƥ Bleðyn . 1107.

CY·CHWEÐYL a·m doðyw o Galch-vynyð :
 Gwarth yn·Eheubarth—an·rheith glodryð.
38 Da ðylei ðyvalei wleð vedyð,
 a llawn vyðei i Ystrad o lad gynnyð.   4
14 Ys llary llywyðei bawb vei yno,
 oni ðaeth penbleth wnaeth arallvro.
15 Am Nest cad gormes tra trach-wres bro ;
 odid o Gymry a·i llavaro.   8
16 Dyved ðy·gyrchei vei va Wyðno,
 ac ni lyvessid Nest niweido :
 Er talu can mu bu erot lo :
18 Go·leith d·yscarant amgant dy vro,   12
 mal y twym huan darth yn yd vo.
19 Ban gyrchad daered ar dir Gwyðno,
 oeð celein vein wen rhwng graean Gro.
21 Ban hwyles echwyð o glyd lwys vro,   16
 nid evrevwys buwch wrthol y llo.

Cadeu Mabon, a Brad Owein . 1116.

23 Cyvarchav Vabon o arall vro !   18
 Caffad, ban amug Owein i vro,
24 cad yn Rhyd y Gors ; cad ar Gowyn :
 cad yng·o·ffyllwyð—affan uðun ;   21
25 cad rhag rhodawl wys—Fftemys erwin,
 i gwaewawr dereu a lleu leïn :
39 cad rhwyvan syberw der·lyw der·lin,   24
 a·i yscwyd yn llaw yng·arthan grŷn
2 A welei Vabon ar vron Rheidawl,
 rhag·ðaw, ar redeg, dy·gymyscawr.
3 Oni bei ac adaneð yð ehettyn,   28
 rhag Mabon, heb galaneð, wy ni·d ëyn
5 O arvod discyn a thervyn cad,
 gwehenid Razo an·o·leithad.   31

To Cadwgan ap Bleðyn.

𝕬 TALE has come to me from Calch-vynyð   ı
    of shame in the South, & of glorious spoil.
He should fare well who conceived a feast of baptism :
    Full should his valley be of increasing blessings.   4
Kindly he governed all who dwelt therein,
    until the entanglement arose—an outsider's work.
The Nest affair brought hardship, over and above local
    explosion : scarcely out of Wales may one speak of it.   8
Dyved would have attacked the land of Gwyðno,
    but it had not dared lest Nest should suffer.
Though fined a hundred cows you had the calf.
Your adversaries are dissolving around your   12
    valley like a mist warmed by the sun.
When the mortuarium was sought on Gwyðno land,
    the corse of the fair lady was under the sands of Gro.
When *Owein* sailed west from a cosy pleasant   16
    home, the cow did not low after the calf.

Griffith ap Rhys, & Owein ap Kadwgan.

I greet Mabon from another valley !   When Owein
ap Cradog was defending his land, we had
    a battle at Rhyd *y Gors* ; a battle on the Cowyn ;   20
    a battle in the darksome thicket —a curse upon it ;
    a battle against the roving horde—the uncouth *Flemish*,
    whose spearmen *Mabon* smote with gleaming lances ;
    a battle with the high-lineaged lord's proud steward,   24
    who, shield in hand, was quaking in the camp.
Those who espied Mabon, on the hillside above
    Rheidol, ran before him pell-mell.
Were it not with wings that they flew,   28
    from Mabon, without slaughter, they would not escape
Between the descent and the end of the war,
    Razo was delivered from destruction.   31

39 Ban *ffo*wys δer*yw* rhag Ilyw y *wl*ad,　　32
　　tavled calch achlwyr o g*rys-grw*ydrad.

8　　*Nu*, nid ev yscavael
　　　i neb δ*y·*δwyn biw moel.
　　Cy·gesclwch, *Gynreinon!*　　36

9　　　rhag gwyr Ileïn rhnδion —
　　　rhag pedrydan dan·δe —

10　　　rhag cadarn gyvwyre —
　　　rhag gwyar er·δygnawd —　　40
　　　rhag avar ystaenawd.　　⊨

11 Cy·chweδyl a·m doδyw o dir*ion* Deheu —
　　traeth rhïeu glew, haelon :

13　ni·th o·gyveirch echwynogion,
　　am ry·gur gwern yng·hadväon.　　45

14 Ban berid *rhyvel* gan Ri Dragon,
　　boIlt na o·wyIl*ted neb* rhag Mabon.

15 O arvod gwr*thun* ! cun δ*y·gwy*δws
　　yng·halaneδ *brad* Ystrad Rwn*ws* :
　　a bu leweny δ iδ *a·i cyrchws.*　　50

17 Bann ymadrawδ gwyr gwedy nnchein
　　cad : ni·s dienghis yscwyd Owein —

18 yscwyd volch wrthiad, yng·had tra·bluδ.
　　Ni ry·*vei* wartheg heb wyneb rhuδ ;　　54

20 a rhuδ eu beudy *wedy·*r mawr vrâd —
　　gor·loched gwyar ar warthav iâd.

21 Ac ar wyneb *ll*wyd yd rhy·gaffad
　　eur-obell greuled, gain i dulliad.　　58

23 Praiδ *Bowys* ioleδ δaresteinad
　　rhag taer vrwydr y tri cyv·estrawn *hâd.*

25 *Wy*, ban gy·vylchyn gainc rhy·scwydad,
　　δis·creinynt *yn* vawr lavnawr am iad. 62

26 Torrad Owein *l*awr o vawr irad :

40 Veinδyδ, *ev* cwyδ*ei vei'*n amwyn gwlad.
　　Ban δiscynn Owein *yng·*wenlad yr

3　Echwyδ, ervyn vnδ o·i Dad.　　66

156

When Mabon's men fled, from the ruler of the place, 32
  their entire armour was discarded in hasty flight.
    Now, it is no credit to anybody
      to carry away defenceless cattle.
    Band together, *ye chieftains*, 36
      againt the men with ruddy lances —
      against general conflagration —
      against a mighty rising —
      against the gore of the conflict — 40
      against the spread of sorrow. ⊢
A story has come to me from the lands of the South —
  from the shore of brave, generous princes.
The aggrieved will not welcome thee,
    because of the hardship of alder battle-grounds. 45
When the Dragon's King caused war to be made,
  (it was) a shock that none felt wild against Mabon.
  By a tragic chance the Dragon fell, in the
  treacherous butchery of Ystrad Rwnws,
    and it was a joy to his attackers. 50
Loud the talk of men after the stress of battle :
  the shield of Owein did not escape — the shield
  that was notched, by resisting, in grievous fight.
Nor, were the cattle without gory faces, 54
  and gory their byre, after the great treachery —
  gore was lodged on the top of their heads.
And over a pallid face was found a finely
  wrought saddle of gold, stained with gore. 58
The *Powysian* herd sought ways of dispersion from
  the persistent attacks of the three alien stocks, who,
  when they forced a breach in a section that swayed,
  brandished wildly their blades about their heads. 62
Owen was cut down from intense hatred :
  At dawn, he was felling defenders of their country.
When Owein is descending into the blessed land of the
  West, he craves for a blessing from his Father. 66

The Battle of Llech Wen.

𝕬M ŵyr*aeth* gwŷr cadr aeth, *y*·gan ᵭyᵭ,   1
  am Wlediᵹ, gweithvuᵭig warthegyᵭ.
56 Urien *ffawd*, hwn an·wawd o·r newyᵭ ;
   cyv·lüeᵭ tëyrneᵭ a·i go*r*vyᵭ.   4
  17 Rhy·vêl*ir* rhwysc en·wir rhwyv bedyᵭ :
    Gwyr Prydein a dwythein yn Ⅼüyᵭ.

  19 *Yn* Ystrad ys dadl cad, cyn y ᵭy*d* ;
    ni noᵭes *y*·mäes na choedyᵭ.   8
  20 Tud achles ᵭy·ormes, pan ᵭyvyᵭ,
    mal tonnawr, tost eu gawr, dros elvyᵭ.

  22 Gweleis wyr, gwych *ged*wyr, yn Ⅼüyᵭ ;
    gwedy *brad* bore câd briwgigyᵭ.   12
  23 Gweleis *drin*—torv teir ffin *yn*·hranc dig ;
    gwaeᵭ god*an*, a·*r* baran go·chlywid.
  25 Yn amwyn Ystrad Gw*y*n y gwelid
    govud *mawr* ang·wyr Ⅼawr, Ⅼuᵭedig.   16

  26 Yn·rws tŷr, gweleis wŷr Ⅼedruᵭion,
57   eirv ᵭiⅬwng y·rag *blwng* gyv·oedion.
    Unyn *yn*·hanc, gan aethant goluᵭion :
  2 Ⅼawᵭ yng·hroes, eu gryd ro*es* ranwynion. 20
    Cyv·edwein i gynrein gywym dôn ;
  4 gwanecawr, Ⅼychant raw*r* eu callon.

    Gweleis *vig* goscorthig bystylad :
    Gweleis waed a vagl*ed* ar ᵭiⅬad.   24
  5 A ᵭuⅬyn ᵭi·av·lym, ᵭwys wrthgad,
    gânt ortho. Ni bu ffo : ban bwyⅬad,
  7 glyw rhy·g*as*, rhy·veᵭas pan veiᵭad.

  8 Gweleis *vig* rhy·o·ᵭig am Urien,   28
    yn ymrysson a·i alon yn ⅠLech Wen.
  9 Yng·henveint galwytheint oeᵭ lawe*n* :
    Aer*awd* wy*d*, go·borthid wrth anghen.
  11 Awyᵭ cad ᵭiffoᵭad yn Urien.   32

Owein ap Cadwgan, slain 1116.

BECAUSE of perfidy, brave men went, at dawn, 1
  against the Gwledig, the victorious cattle-lifter.
Owein's *fate* will be a fresh cause of shame :
  The joint action of the princes will overthrow him. 4
The baptized ruler's evil career shall be utterly crushed.
  The men of Prydein will leap into action.

At Ystrad the strife began before daybreak :
  (Owein) gave quarters neither afield, nor in the woods. 8
He devours the fat of the land as he goes : like
  baleful-sounding billows (he sweeps) over the country.

I saw men, fine *warriors*, in battle array : after the
  morning's treachery, their mangled bodies were found. 12
I saw a *battle* : the host of three confines, in the hateful
  grip of death, raise a shout, & the rage (of war) is heard.
In defence of Ystrad Gwyn had been seen *the great*
  tribulation of the poor sons of the soil, exhausted. 16

At the portal of the towers, I had seen blood-stained
  men who drop their arms before their angry fellows.
They made peace, for they went into the interiors ;
  Solaced in misfortune their shout causes blanched cheeks.
(Owein's) chieftains know the triumphant note ; *as* 21
  it is poured forth, they hide the tumult in their hearts.

I witnessed the spite of the wrathful retinue's activity,
  and the blood that was sprinkled on their mail. 24
They planned a sharp, severe attack, and take
  cover.   There was no flight : upon reflection
  the behated prince wondered that he was challenged.

I saw the animus of the spite around Owein, 28
  contending with his enemies at ILech Wen.
(Still) in the thick of the wrath of war he was cheerful.
  The lust of slaughter was satisfied as fate decreed :
  Eagerness for battle was quenched in Owein. 32

Armes Prydein.

DYS·CO·GAN Awen *Ffreinc* ðy·vryssyn — 1
marhaneð a meueð hêd genhyn.
13 A phennaeth ehalaeth IFra*w* unbyn,
4 wedy heð, ðy·anheð bob mehyn. 4
Gwyr gwychr yn trydar gasnar d*rei*syn :
6 Escud yng·ovud, rhy·hyd ðiffyn.
Gwaethl *Mwng* wyr Gweryð ; gwascar *i* Allmyn
8 wnahawnt or·voleð ; gwedy, gwehyn. 8
A chymod Cymry a gwyr Dulyn —
9 Gwyðyl *rhy·ðoethon* Von, a Phrydyn.
Cornyw achlud*yn* gynn·wys genhyn :
11 Ad·borion vyð Brython ban ðy·orvyn. 12
Bell amser, dyo·ganher, dybyðyn
13 tëyrneð o vonheð, *a* orescyn
wyr Gogleð yng·hynteð eu cylchyn —
14 ym·herveð eu tac*h*weð y discynnyn. 16

Dys·go·gan Myrðin cyvervyðhyn,
16 Yn Aber yðon, meiron tëyrn.
A chyn ni bei raith, llaith a gwynyn :
17 O ewyllis vryd yd wrthvynnyn. 20
Meiron eu tretheu ðy·chynnullyn ;
19 yng·hedoeð Kymry ni·d *vi* delhyn.
Yssyð ðyledawg a ðywawd i·n
na ðyffei a dalei, yng·heith, *ðim.* 24

Vab Mair l mawr o air, pryd na tharðed
22 rhag·bennaeth Saeson, weison hoffeð.
Pell bwy y cylchyn y·wrth dëyrn Gwyneð —
Ev gyrhawd Allmyn i alltudeð ; 28
24 neb ni·s arhaeðwy ðyffwy yn·aer.
Ni wys py·r dreiglynt ym·hob aber.
26 Ban brynwyd Daned, drwy ffed calleð,
gan Hors a Hengys — ing eu rhysseð. 32

𝕿𝖍𝖊 𝕻𝖗𝖔𝖕𝖍𝖊𝖈𝖞 𝖔𝖋 𝕻𝖗𝖞𝖉𝖊𝖎𝖓.

𝕿HE Muse prophesies that the *French* will hie away —
that their folk with their property will fly with them —
that the widespread supremacy of the *Aberffro* Princes 3
will extend everywhere, when peace has come.
The stalwarts will loudly hate the marauders :
He, who rushes into trouble, will have a long defence. 6
Magnus will attack the men of Dee ; *his* Northmen will
scatter them at their triumphal feast ; he will, then, depart.
And the Kymry will make peace with the men of Dublin —
the Gwyδyl *who had come* to Mon and Prydyn. 10
The Cornovi will carry natives away with them ;
Remnants will the Brythons be when they triumph.
At a distant time, it is prophesied, there will come 13
high-born princes, who will overcome .
the men of Gogleδ at the centre of their circuit —
in the middle of their retreat they will fall. 16

𝕸yrδin prophesies that the stewards of the King
will meet at Aber Yδon ; and before there
could be any right (the Kymry) will complain of a levy,
against which they will, heart and soul, protest 20
that the stewards will gather their crops, since
in Kymry's treasuries there will be no reserve.
A great authority has told us that no one would
ever come, who should pay anything in bondage. 24

𝕾on of Mary, of puissant power, may the time never
arise for the supremacy of the Saxons, sons of greed.
Far be their border from the Prince of Gwyneδ,
who will drive the Northmen into exile : 28
May none he fails to seize escape the grave.
It is not known why they wander in every bay :
When Thanet was secured, through manifest wisdom,
by Hors and Hengist — straightened were their means. 32

14 Eu cynnyδ y·wrthym : ys an·vonheδ,   33
  2 wedy rhyn, dilein ceith y·mynwer.
  3 Dy·chyvyd anghen angheu Ilawer :
  2 Dy·chyvyd meδdawd mawr wirawd meδ : 36
  4 Dy·chyvyd aereu δagreu gwrageδ :
  5 Cyffry etgyIlaeth bennaeth Iled·ffer :
    Dy·chyvyd tristid byd o ry·her
  7 ban vyδ *Normanieid* an tëyrneδ.   40
    Gwrthottid Trindawd δyrnawd bwyIler —
  8 dilein o Saeson Vrython anheδ.
    Boed gynt *a*·u rheges yn alltudeδ,
10 no myned Kymry yn δi·vröeδ.   44

    Vab Mair, mawr o *ras*, pryd na·s terδyn
11 Gymry, rhag göeir brehyr unbyn ?
    Cynrycheid eilweith *an*·rheith gŵynyn —
13 un gor, un gynghor, un eisor ynt.   48
    Ni *vy*δ, er mawreδ, na·s Ileverynt ;
15 nag er hepcor *cas* na·s cymodynt.
    I Đuw a Dewi dym·orchmynnynt :
16 Talent *ged, pallent* ffled i AIlmyn :   52
    Gwnaent an·eireu eiseu trevδyn.
    Saeson a Chymry gyvervyδyn :
    y·am lan *Dwy*, treul*yn drwy* ym·wrthryn.
19 O δirvawr vyδin yδ ym·brovyn :   56
    ac ý·am aIlt Ilavnawr ang·awr a gryn :
20 A amwyn Geir*iog* ergyr verw Ilyn ;
    a Ilym aw*r* a δaw, a garw δiscyn ;
22 ac mal baläon Saeson syrthyn.   60
    Cynyrcheid Kymry, cyv·un δuIlyn ;
23 blaen wrth vôn granwynnion, cyvyngyn.
    Yng·warth gevyneu meirion greinhyn,
25 a·u byδin yng·waedlin yn eu cylchyn.
    EreiII, ar eu traed, trwy goed cilhyn .   65

Their prosperity comes from us : it is, *therefore*,   33
  churlish to destroy so soon serfs under the yoke.
Want will cause the death of many :
Much mead-liquor will give rise to drunkenness :
Battles will give rise to women's tears :   37
Wailing will affect the feeble chieftain :
A world-sadness will arise, from insubordination,
  when the *Normans* shall be our lords.   40
The Trinity will avert the blow that is meditated—
  the destruction of the Brython home by the Saxons.
Sooner be he, who has cursed them, in exile
  than that the Kymry should lose their land.   44

Gracious son of Mary, when would not the Kymry
  rise against the abuse of the baron-chiefs ?
Our representatives, a united band, of one mind
  and lot, will complain a second time of plunder.   48
There is nothing, by way of magniloquence, they will
  not say ; nor, to avoid ill-feeling, they will not agree to.
To God and Dewi they commit themselves : they   51
  will pay tribute, but refuse a domicile to the Allmyn,
  who will create disturbances from want of a home.
The Saxons & the Kymry will meet beyond the banks
  of the *Dee* : they will wear out by contention.   55
With a great army they will prove each other ; & beyond *Berwyn* the spearmen will tremble miserably.
He, who will defend the Ceir*iog*, will contend with a
  boiling flood : a shrill war-cry will come, & a fearsome descent : like blossoms will the Saxons fall.   60
Kymry's men will form as one body ; close to the
  rear of the pale-faced *foes* their van will hem them in.
In the disgrace of gyves the stewards will cringe—
  & their army in a pool of blood will surround them.
Others, on foot, through the woods will retreat ;   65

15 Drwy Vwlch y Dinas Voras ffohyn.   66
    Rhyvel ni ðym·chwel i dir Prydyn :
 2 Attor glaw gynghor—mal mor Ilithryn.

ⓂⒺeirIon Caer Geri di·vri gwynant ;   69
 4 rhai·r dyffryn, rhai·r bryn ni·s dir·wadant.
    Yn Aber Yðon ni vad ðoethant ;
 5 anaeleu dretheu, dy·chynullant :   72
    Naw ugein canhwr y dis·cynnant—
 7 Mawr watwar ! namyn pedwar ni·d atcorant.
    Dy·heð i·w gwrageð a ðywedant—
 8 eu crysseu yn Ilawn creu a or·olchant.   76
 9 *Gwyneð* gynyrcheid, eneid ði·chwant,
    wŷr Deheu *rhag* tretheu a amygant.
11 Ilym-liveid lavnawr, Ilwyr y Ilaðant :
    Ni vyd meðig mwyn o·r a wnäant.   80
12 Byðinoeð gwaladr cadr y deuant ;
    dyrchavwynt *eu gwlad, bob* cad a wnant.
14 *Ar hynt* an·o·leith yð *ym·ðeith*ant ;
    yn gorffen tretheu angheu wðant.   84
15 Ereill, ar ostri, a ry·blanhant,
    ac yn oes oeseu ni·s escorant.
    Yng·hoed, y·maes, *ym·ro*, ym·ryn,
17 *ev* gerð yn·howyll ganhwyll genhyn.   88
    Cynan a rag·wan ym·hob discyn :
    Saeson rhag Brython gwae a gênyn.
19 Kadwaladr yn baladr gan i unbyn ;   91
    drwy synhwyr, yn Ilwyr, *ev* a·u dichlyn.
21 Ban syrthwynt yng·hlas dros eu herchwyn,
    dagreu custuð rêd ar ruð Allmyn.   94
23 yng·orffen ang·reith an·rheith dengyn.
    Sais â i hynt Gaer Wynt, pwy gynt *t*rechynt :
24 Gwyn eu byd, Gymry, ban adroðynt.   97
    Rhy·n·gwarawd Trindawd o·r trallawd gynt.

Through the Pass of Dinas to Boras they will flee. 66
War will not return to the land of Prydyn : Rain will
upset all plans : like the flood, the *foes* will glide away.

The stewards of Caer Geri will lament ingloriousness :
Some the dale, some the hill will not disdain. 70
Unto Aber Yδon they will not come for their good :
Terrible tribute they will collect—
Nine score centuries they will be descending— 73
O the mockery ! there will return but four. These
will report great tranquillity to their wives, *while*
their garments, soaked in gore, they will be washing.
The uncovetous soul of the *Gwyneδ* representatives 77
will defend the men of the South from *paying* tribute.
Sharply-ground blades do kill outright, and
no compassionate healer can make alive again. 80
The armies of our Prince will bravely advance :
May they glorify their country in every fight.
On a very destructive *expedition* they will go :
in putting an end to tributes they will taste death. 84
Fresh levies they will impose in the form of hospitality,
which never, never will be set aside.
In forest and field, in dale, and on hill, this
(hospitality) will attend them *as a* lamp in darkness. 88
Kynan will lead the attack in every descent :
Brythons will cause the Saxons to sing songs of woe.
Kadwaladr will be a pillar with his chieftains, 91
whom, for their ability alone, he will select.
When the Allmyn fall into a district beyond their bor-
der, in custody their cheeks will run with tears. 94
After a successful onslaught the villeins will pillage.
The Saxon will go to Winchester after vanquishment.
Blessed the Kymry, when they shall tell these things.
The Trinity will deliver us from our former trouble. 98

Na chryned Dyved na Glywyssing :   99
16 Ni·s gwnahon volawd meirion tëyrn,
 1   na chynghor Saeson, ceffyn obryn.
    Ni·s gwna go·veðud veðdawd genhyn.
 3 Heb ðal, yd roð*eint* vaint a geffyn
    i ymðiveid, gweð*won*, a *thlodion* ryn.   104
 5 Drwy eiriawl Dewi a sein Prydyn,
    hyd Ffrwd ar L*air*go ffohawd Aỻmyn.

 Ðys·go·gan Awen dy·ðaw y dyð,
 7 ban ðyffo ỻwys, yng·wŷs *rhïyð*,   108
    *y*n gôr un gynghor— Ỻoegr lüosyð,
    er gobeith ann·eir ar·n prydawl lüyð :
 9 A cherð araỻvro, a ffo beunyð :
    Ni ŵyr rhuð ym*l*að cwð â, cwð vyð.   112
 11 Dy·chyrchwynt gyvarth, mal arth o wyð,
    i dalu gwyneith, gwaed eu henyð.
 12 Ad·vi beleitral—*gwyar* ðiỻyð ;
    ni·d arbettwy car gorff i gilyð.   116
    Ad·vi ben gwaỻawg heb e*nei*nyð :
 14 Ad·vi wrageð gweðw a meirch gweilyð :
    Ad·vi ubein uthr rhag rhuthr *rheinyð* :
 16 Ỻïaws ỻav*n* a phar wascar lüyð ;   120
    cennadeu angheu, dy·chyvervyð.
    *C*an saffwynt *yng·had* wrth eu henyð,
 18 ev dïalawr ar·werth y dreth beunyð ;
    a·r *aml* gennadeu, a·r geu lüyð.   124

 20 Ðy·*dy*rvir Kymry—cyv·ergyr*ant*
    yn gyt·ffyð, gyd·eir, gyweir *y*ð *ant*.
 21 Dy·dyrvir Kymry i beri *gwysi*ant ;
    a ỻwyth, ỻïaws gwlad, a gynuỻant.   128
 23 Ỻuman glan Ðewi a ðyrchavant,
    i rysiaw Gwyðyl : drwy li eingant
 24 a·*r* Gynhon Dulyn : Genhym savant,
    ban ðyffont i·r gad, ni·d ym·wadant.   132

166

Dyved and Glywyssing need have no fear : 99
  Those who will not praise the King's stewards, nor
  do the bidding of the Saxon, shall have their reward.
Mead-drinking leads not to drunkenness with them.
Without reservation they will distribute all they get
  among orphans, widows, and *the poor* not a few. 104
By the intercession of Dewi and the saints of Prydyn,
  as far as Portlaw on the Suir the Northmen will flee.

℘he Muse prophesies that a day will come, when
  the Gewissi will answer the summons of the King, 108
  a unanimous company—England's forces—in the
  hope of bringing disgrace on our timely hosting.
It will traverse strange districts & daily flee : active 111
  warfare knows not its course, nor what will happen.
They will make for the barking, like a bear from the
  wood, to avenge the blood of their ancestors. 114
There will be spear-thrusts, and flow of blood ; even
  a friend will not spare the body of his fellow :
There will be a chief lost without an *anointer* :
There will be widows, and riderless horses : 118
There will be a fearful outcry at the onset of the
  lancers : the countless blades & javelins will scatter
  the host, whom the angels of death will intercept. 121
Since they will stand in war by their kin,
  the farming of the tribute will be avenged daily,
  upon the many collectors and the traitorous host. 124

℘he Kymry will be roused—they will strike together :
  confident, unanimous, prepared *they will go.*
The Kymry will be roused to mobilize ; & the nation,
  in the plenitude of its numbers, will assemble. 128
They will raise the banner of holy Dewi to con-
  found the Gwyδyl, who will escape by water to the
  Northmen of Dublin.   Those who stay behind,
  when they come to battle, will not hold back. 132

Govynnan i·r Saeson py geisant :   133

17 Pwy vaint yn·yled o·r wlad Ꝺaliant ?

   Cw mae eu hely*th*—pan seilassant ?

  2 Cw mae eu ceneꝺl—pan y doethant ?   136

  3 Er *oed* Gwrthĕyrn *arnom* sathrant :

   ni cheffir gwir randir a·n carant.

  4 Neu, breinheu a·n Sant rhy·sanghassant—

   rheitheu *Ty*-Ꝺewi rhy·dorassant.   140

  6 Ym·gedwynt Gymry. Ban ym·welant,

   ni·d ahont Allmyn o·r van savant,

  8 *nes* caffont seith-weith werth Ꝺigonsant ;

   neu angheu dïeu yng·wrth eu c*hw*ant.   144

  9 Ev talhawr an·war Armawn garant

   am drais a gormes escorassant

 10 ym·hedeir blyneꝺ ar bedwar cant.

   Gwyr gwychrion, wallt hir, er·gyr*ch* do*nn*yꝺ—

 11 i ꝺi·hol Saeson o *V*on ꝺyvyꝺ.   149

   Dybi o *Lairges* lynghes rewyꝺ—

 13 rhewiniawd yn g*wl*ad—rhwygawd llüyꝺ.

   Dybi o Alclud wyr drud, gweiryꝺ,   152

 14 ꝺihol o Brydein virein lüyꝺ.

   Dybi oludawg braw gyweithyꝺ—

 16 cedwyr y·ar gadveirch—ni pheirch i henyꝺ.

   Saeson o bopparth yng·warth ꝺeubyꝺ :   156

 17 rhy·drenghi*t* eu hoes, ni·s di·oes *rh*yꝺ.

   Dy·ꝺeubi a'ngheu·r Du Gyweithyꝺ :

   clevyd a weryꝺ a·u rhy·ꝺiffyꝺ.

 19 Gwedy cur, gorian, a chanhwynyꝺ,   160

   boed berth a·n differth yng·wrth dryg·ffyꝺ :

 21 Boed vur am·gor a·n cyffyllwyꝺ :

   Boed greu, boed angheu eu cyweithyꝺ.   164

 23 *Ev* a Chadwaladr, cadr yn llüyꝺ,

   edmyccawr hyd vrawd, ffawd a ꝺeubyꝺ.

They will demand of the Saxons what they are seeking :
  How much of the land they hold in fee ?   134
  Where is their stock—when was it founded ?
  Where are their people—whence did they come ?
  Since the time of Gwrtheyrn they trample upon us : 137
  We cannot enjoy the rightful share of our heritage.
  And now, they have trampled on the prerogatives of our
  Saint, and disregarded the rights of *St.* David's.   140
Let the Kymry be on guard.   When they visit us, the
  Allmyn will not quit the place in which they settle,
  until they get seven times the value of their work ;
  or meet with certain death in return for their greed. 144
The barbarous Northern race will be paid
  for the oppression and plunder it carried on
  during four years and four hundred.
Brave, long-haired, men will rush the waves,   148
  and will come to expel the Saxons out of Mon.
From Portlaw will come a wanton fleet,
  which will ruin our country, and rend our host.
There will come from Alclyde bold rustics   152
  who will expel from Prydein a magnificent host.
There will come a prince who will prove the allies—
  warriors, on their steeds, whose race he will not respect.
The Saxons, on every side, will fall into disgrace—   156
  their time will come to an end, but freedom will endure.
The Dark allies will surely come to their death—
  the plague that will spring up will extinguish them.
After anxiety, the war-cry & the conflict, let him   160
  be prosperous, who defended us against bad faith :
  Let him be the fence-wall around us & our comfort :
  Let him shed blood & bring death to the allies.
He & Cadwaladr, valiant in warfare, will be   164
  admired till doom ; fortune will favour them.

25 Deu unben dengyn, dwys gyn*ghaw*syδ, 166
 Saeson or·sengyn, pleidyn Ðovyδ.
 Deu hael, deu ge*i*dwa*d* gwlad warthegyδ,
18 di·archar, parawd, unffawd, unffyδ.
 Deu erchwyn Prydein virein lüyδ ; 170
2 deu a·r ni·s gwna gwarth, *p*arch*av* beunyδ.

Ɗys·go·gan derwyδ vaint a δervyδ : 172
4 O Vanaw hyd Lydaw i·w Ilaw vyδ—
 O Ðyved hyd Ðaned wy bieuvyδ—
6 O Wawr hyd Weryδ, a·i haber*yδ*,
 Ilettawd eu pennaeth dros yr Echw*yδ*. 176
 Attora*n* Gynhon ; Saeson ni vyδ :
8 At·chwelwynt Wyδyl a·r eu henyδ :
 rhy·δyrchwynt Gymry gadr gy·weithyδ.
10 Byδinoeδ am·gor athor *lüyδ*, 180
 a thëyrneδ dwys gedwys eu ffyδ.
 Ði wys pob Ilynghes a thres δervyδ ;
12 a chymod cyn*r*an gan i gilyδ.
 Ni alwawr Gynhon yn gynivy*δ* 184
14 namyn cy*r*ch Cadwaladr gynniweir*yδ*.
 Eil Gymro, Ilawen a Ilavar vyδ ;
 am ynys bwyeid haid a δervyδ.
16 Ban *wnant* galaneδ *ar* eu henyδ, 188
 hyd yn*g·H*aer Santwig *c*wynedig vyδ.
18 Allmyn a·r·gychwyn yn alltudyδ,
 ol wrth ol atcor ar eu henyδ.
19 Saeson wrth angor, ar vor beunyδ ; 192
 Kymry wenerawl, wrawl ɔrvyδ.
21 Na cheisw*ch* lyvrawr angawr brydyδ—
 Armes yr Ynys namyn hyn ni byδ.
22 Jolwn Ri grëwys nev ac elvyδ : 196
 Boed tywys Dewi i·r cynivyδ.
24 Yn yr ing gwell no dim dwyv*awl* ffyδ :
 ni threinc, ni δ*i*einc, ni·d ar·δispyδ—
25 ni wyw, ni wellyg, ni phlyg, ni chryδ. 200

These two leaders of the people, deep of counsel   166
  will trample on the Saxons, and support the Lord.
Two generous ones—protectors of the land of cattle ;
  irrepressible, equipped, of one faith, and fortune.
Two bulwarks of Prydein's magnificent army—two   170
  who do no ignoble thing, I shall ever respect them.

The sage prophesies what great things will happen :
  From Man to Brittany they will hold : from   173
  Dyved to (the forest of) Dean they will possess :
From Woore to the Dee, and *thence* to its mouths
  their sovereignty will spread over the West.   176
The Northmen will be thrust back ; Saxons will flee :
  The Gwyδyl will return to their own people :
  The Kymry will extol them, their brave allies.
The armies of the border, our host will break up,   180
  and our sage princes will keep their faith.
Against our people every fleet & trouble will disap-
  pear : our chieftain will make peace with his fellow.
The Northmen will not be called combatants,   184
  but the gathering of Cadwaladr's tourists.
The other Kymro, (*O.G.*) merry and jubilant will be :
  Around the battered island a horde will perish.   187
When they make a murderous attack upon their kin,
  there will be sorrowing as far as Kaer (Gybi)'s
  Holy Bay. The Northmen will fly as exiles,
  and retrace their course to their own people.   191
The Saxons will remain at sea, riding at anchor ;
  and the venerable brave Kymry will conquer.
Search not the books of a miserable bard—   194
  there will be no other Prophecy about the Island.
Let us worship the Father who created Heaven & earth :
Let (St.) David be a guide to the combatants.
In distress there is nothing like holy faith :   198
  it dies not, deserts not, is not exhausted ; it does
  not faint, nor fail, nor turn aside, nor waste away.

Darontwy.

O UW nev ðifferwy,　　　1
　　rhag Ꝉanw Ꝉed orðwy.
28 Cyntav *y* tarrwy,
23　a dreis dros Ðovrdwy.
　　Py *d*ren a vo vwy　　　5
24　nog *yn* Daronwy ?
　　Ni·d vi a·n noðwy,
25　*b*an gyrch Balch nevwy.　8
　　Ys rhin y suðwy—
26　gwanawr gwyr Cornwy.
　　Odid a·i gwypwy—
　　hudlath Vathonwy.　　　12
29 Yng·hoed pan tyffwy—
　　ffrwytheu nwy cymrwy.
2　A·r lan Gwyꝉionwy,
　　Kynan a·i caffwy,　　　16
　　pryd pan wledychwy.
3　Dy·ðeuant etwaeth,
　　dros drei a thros draeth,
4　bedeir priv bennaeth :　20
　　A·r bymhed, ni·d gwaeth—
5　gwyr gwrð ehalaeth,
　　a·r Brydein arvaeth.
6　Gwrageð a vi ffraeth :　24
　　Eiꝉon a vi caeth :
　　Rhyverthwy hîr aeth,
7　a veð warogaeth.
　　Dy·ðaw dwy rïein—　　28
8　Gweðw a gwriawg vain :
　　Ꝉedyn eu hadein
　　ar wyr yn goriein.　　　31
9　Dy·ðeuant, gynrein,
　　o am dir Prydein ;

Daronwy.

AY God of heaven defend (us)   1
    against the rising tide of violence.
First may He strike him,
    who will pillage beyond the Dee.   4
What insolence can be greater,
    than that *at* Daronwy?   There
    will be none to protect us when
    the Proud one enters the sanctuary.
'Tis a secret that *Hugh* will sink—   9
    that the Cornovi will be dispatched.

Scarcely may any know
    the magic wand of Mathonwy.   12
In the wood where it is growing,
    its fruits none may take.
On the banks of Gwyllionwy
    may Kynan find it,   16
    at the time when he rules.
Over ebb and strand four
    sovereign powers will yet   20
    again come upon the fifth,
    which is not inferior—
    upon brave, generous men,
    who rule over Prydein's lot.
The women will be violated :   24
    Strangers will be made captive :
Prolonged pressure of adversity
    will secure submission.
Two queens will come—   28
    a widow and a married fair one :
They will extend their protection
    over men in dire stress.
Leaders will come, from   32
    beyond the land of Prydein ;

29   Eu cerδed gyngein ;   33

10   Eu gwawd a yscein.

     Anan δerw a drain :

     a·r gorδ yd gyngein.   37

11 *Gnawd* ci i rynnu ; march i ryniaw;

     Eidon i wan ; hwch i dyr*iaw* :

12 Pymhed, ꟿwdn gwyn — a*b*erth Jesu,

     a wisc Aδav, o·i ymatru.   41

4 *Bwystvi*led coed cain eu syꟿu,

     hyd yd vuant, a hi*r* yd vu.

15 Ban wnel Kymry ỳ cam-hüalu,

     ceir araꟿ vro pwy carho nu.   45

16 ꟿesteireis gam, gor·gam eglwg :

     ꟿe cewsit da ni·r gaho drwg.

     Mygedorth Rhun ys ev amlwg,   48

18   rhwng Caer Rïein a Chaer Rynwg —

     rhwng Din Eiδin a Din Eiδwg :

19   eglur dremyn a wŷl golwg.   50

     Rhag tan rhynawd dychyffrwy mwg.

20   A·n Rhëen, Duw, a·n rhy amwg.   ꟾ

       Ꙍwawd ꟿugδd mawr.

      CATHLEU *d*arogant   1
         *sei*th nieu nodant :—

   74 Dyw ꟿun dy·byδant ;

      i beithaw yδ ant.   4

    14 Dyw Mawrth, yd rannant

      wŷth i·w hyscarant.

      Dyw Merchyr, med*r*ant

      ry·odres ry·chwant.   8

    16 Dyw Ieu, escorant

      eiδolyδ an·chwant.

    17 Dyw Gwener, gormant

      yng·waed go·noviant.   12

Their advance will be in unison ;   34
Their fame will spread.
They will attack oak and thorn
   (*fences*) : The nation will rejoice.   37
The dog *is wont* to shiver ; the horse to shy ;
   the bull to gore ; the sow to upturn the soil :
The fifth, the sacrifice of Christ, a white
   beast will clothe Adam, by fleecing it.   41
Beasts of the forests, lovely the sight of them,
   while they flourished, and long that was.
When the Kymry will wrongly fetter them,
   a stranger will be found who loves them still.
I checked wrong, manifest great wrong :   46
   Where you find good you will not find evil.
The funeral pile of Rhun is conspicuous,
   twixt Maiden and Beeston castles —
   twixt Din Eiðin and Din Eiðwg :   50
a clear vision will catch a glimpse of it.
Shortly before there is fire a smoke rises.
May our sovereign God protect us.   ⵊ

The Great Hosting.

THE prophetic songs   1
   specify seven days :—
Monday, they will come ;
   to scout they will go.   4
Tuesday, they will impart
   discontent to their foes.
Wednesday, they will display
   the pomp of excess.   8
Thursday they will indulge
   their idols of lust.
Friday, in abundance
   of blood they will wade.   12

74 Dyw Sadwrn, *swynant* ;   13
   a·u meirwon gladant.

18 Dyw Sul, yn geugant
   dïeu dy·*m·chwel*ant.   16

20 Pym IIong a phym cant,
   o *rith*ad noviant.
   O brithi rith*es*,
21   ni·*d* oes n*i* ved*r*i.   20
   O rith Brithoni,
   ysedig e*i*ồi—
22 eil coed c*l*og*w*yni :
   Antareồ ồy·bi.   24
   Pawb ồi adon ä*e*i ;
   ar Weryồ cwymp*e*i.

23 D*rywon* ồarogaᴡn   27
   wae hir rhag Garmawn.
24 Hir, cylch oeồ gynghan
   i·n gwaladr, ach *C*ynan.
25 Pyd, *o* byồ bychan,
   ồiva wrês hüan.   32

26 Dys·co·gan derwyồ :—
   "A vu a ồyvyồ."
   Wybr eir gerồ Ðovyồ—
75 cerồ*l*awn ynghenyồ.   36
   Wylhawd eil echwyồ
2 yn·horroeồ mynyồ.
   Ban *vy*ồ beu IIawn hyồ,
   Brithion a·r gynhyồ.   40
3 I Vriþion dybi
   waeồ Wyneồ o·vri.
4 Gwedy aur r*e*nni
   diffeithan Moni,   44
   Llŷn, ac Eryri—
5 anheồ*ant* ynồi.

Saturday, *they will consult the*   13
  oracles, and bury their dead.
Sunday, inevitably,
  they will verily return.   16
Five ships and five hundred,
  by enchantment float.
If you colour what he enchanted   19
  there is nothing you cannot attain.
By the enchantment of the Scotti,
  consumed is the ivy—   22
  the fosterling wood of the cliffs :
  Mad fury will follow.
Every one against his lord would go :
  on the Dee, he would fall.
The druids predict a long   27
  misery on account of Wexford.
This haunt had long been friendly
  to our leader, of the line of Kynan.
Ill-feeling, though it be little,   31
  destroys the warmth of the sun.
The druid prophesies that,
  what has been, will be.   34
The sky pours forth the Lord's song—
  full of music, its undertones.
The Fosterling of the West will weep
  in the recesses of the mountain.   38
When the country is full of deer,
  the Scotti will increase.
To the Scotti will come the
  appeal of renowned Gwyneδ.   42
After you distribute gold,
  they will lay waste Mon,
ILŷn, & Snowdonia,
  and will dwell therein.   46

75 Dys·co·gan perffeith — 47
   anheδyn δiffeith.
6 Cymry, bedeir iaith,
   symudant i hareith. 50
7 I·t dyvi vuwch vraith
   a wnaho gwyneith :
8 Veinδyδ a vrevawd, 53
   veinoeth y berwhawd :
   Ac ar dir verwhawr,
9 yn ℿongoeδ yssawr. 56
   Cathl gwae cenhitor,
10 cylch Prydein amgor.
   Ant, o un gynghor,
11 yng·wrthol warth mor. 60
   Boed gwir eu myned —
   Tragwyδawl, byδ*ed* !
12 Dorwys δ·olℿynghid
   o δovaeth eith*l*yd. 64
   Cyvran ℿawn *tristid,*
13 yd gyvarch gywid.
   Heb ebawl aeav —
   Heb henvon hâv — 68
14 Heb o·vur *gobeith,*
   byd a vyδ diffeith.
   Direid tynghettor ;
   y grog a·u *hescor.* 72
15 Hoiw gweδ trwy grevyδ :
   Gwyrein bron drwy ffyδ :
16 Terwynn tuth i jolyδ,
   i hewyd ar vedyδ. 76
17 Ni wân cyℿeℿawr
   veiwyr cleδyvawr.
18 Ni·d oeδ uδu y puchyssyn —
   anaw angerδawl trevδyn. 80

Most true the prophecy—   47
  they will dwell in the wilderness.
They will change the speech
  of Kymry, with its four languages.
To thee will come the brindled cow,
  which will work deliverance.   52
At dawn it will low ;
  at eve it will seethe :
What will be boiled on land
  will be eaten aboard ships.   56
The song of woe shall be chanted
  around Prydein's border.
They will, of one accord,
  return athwart the sea.   60
True be it that they are going ;
  Forever let it be !
He entreated that he be set free
  from a painful durance.   64
A lot full of sadness
  eagerly seeks friendship :
Without a horse in winter :
Without a cow in summer :   68
Without the buffer of hope
  the world becomes a wilderness.
The wicked will be exorcised :
  the Cross will deliver them.   72
Bright the countenance of the pious :
  Exalted the breast through faith :
The fervent speeds to the act of
  worship, intent on baptism.   76
Those armed with a dagger cannot
  pierce warriors armed with swords.
They had not what they desired—
  the intense inspiration of a home.   80

75 A ryˑŵyr gareð Creuðyn—y Gwyðyl, 81
   aˑr Eingl, *a gwyr* Prydyn :
20 *Saeson* gyvred ar ðiscyn,
21 o Wynvynyð—o Hirmyn   84
Dygedawr gwyðveirch *hyd* ar lyn Gogleð ;
   *i Ar*ꝉechweð *y cyrchyn* :
22 Y cas wyr o glas *Du*lyn—
   o echen a*ch*as henyn.   88
Dygedawr drwy *li* ðyˑgyrchyn vranhes,
   a orˑgoðes wyr ein*ym* :
24 Yˑmeryð miled seithyn,
   aˑr mor agor *am* gryssyn,   92
26 heb erˑglywaw arawd nebawd vehyn
   *y*ˑ*gan* vynawg, *neu vrawd.*
25   Uch o vor, uch o vo*ryn*,
   uch o orr ynial ebyrn—   96
   coed, mäes, tyno, a bryn.
    76   Yd ðyvi brithred
       ꝉꝉïaws gynired :
     2   Govud am wehyn   100
       ðïal *Duw ernyn* !
       Drwy hoiw gar*d*odeu
     3   *yn i* breswyl*vaeu*,
       Creawdr cyvoethawg   104
       a vaðeuˑth bechawd.
     4   Peꝉꝉ, cyn no dyðbrawd,
       y daw diwarnawd
       a ðiˑwŷr ðaer ffawd—   108
       a dervyn drei*s*on
       o dir ꝉwerðon.
     6   Yna, ymˑHrydein   111
       y daw dadwyrein—
       Brython o vonheð
       a rw*yv* yngˑ*Wyne*ð.   114

The Gwyδyl, the Angle, & the men of Prydyn
   will know well the crime of Creuδyn :   82
Saxons flock together into the attack,
   from Gwynvynyδ and Long Mynd.   84
Ships will be brought as far as Gogleδ water —
   to Arllechweδ they will repair :
Hateful the men from the clan of Dublin —
   from a hated origin they descend.   88
By sea will be brought those who will attack the
   forces, which have so harassed our men :
In the plashes they will shoot the horses :
The sea will open about those who rush in
without their hearing prayers at any place   93
   from monk *or brother*.
Their cry will rise from sea and breaker,
   and the recess of a wood-bank wild —   96
aye, from wood and field, and dale and hill.
      There will come the turmoil
        of numerous expeditions :
      But the chagrin of evacuating   100
        God will visit on them.
      By cheerful offerings,
        in His tabernacles,
        the puissant Creator   104
        will remit thy sins.
      Long ere doomsday
        will come a time, which
        will un-crook earth's lot ;   108
        and end incursions
        from the land of Erin.
      Then, in Prydein,   111
        will become ascendant
        a Brython by descent,
        who will rule in Gwyneδ :   114

76 A bi barn o ꝺyꝺ   115
  ang·hyngres *lluyꝺ*.
 Go·gan sywyꝺon
  ing colledigion : 118
 9 Go·gan derwyꝺon,
  "Tra mor tra Brython."
 Hav ni byꝺ hinon :
10 Byrhawr brëyron : 122
  a·u deubyꝺ gwan*g*red :
11 Tra merin *c*ad cêd.
 Mil ymbrawv Brydein urꝺin :
 Ac *ry*·am·gyffrwn gy·ffin 126
 ni chwynav : ym·ogled wern—
13 Gwerni weꝺ waelod uffern.
 Ergryni*r* cyllestrig gaen 129
14 gan wledig gwlad an·orffen.

ᚦ ᚦ ᚦ

Am a ꝺy·ꝺyvi.

ꝲN wir dy·ꝺyvi rhwyv a vi gâr ; 1
 odid o vab dyn *welyn* i bâr.
76 Rhy·glywhawr rhagꝺaw maw gyvagar ;
 Byꝺin a gwaedlin a ry·escar. 4
18 Ot rhy·ganer kyrn gwerin dringar,
 rhy·thrych rhy·gyrchynt yng·hleꝺyval.
 Brein ac eryron olych wyar, 7
20 ac, ar lwybr gwrid*goch*, wrys di·archar.
 Ar·ꝺyrch e*v*, waladr, lu *cadr*, llachar,
22 ac wyneb vyꝺin bröyꝺ ynial.

ꝲN wir dy·ꝺyvi ymrysoneu : 11
23 Govuned dyngant yng·hyn·echreu
 blwyꝺyn, yd vuꝺid rhi hyd draetheu.

And he will be a law-giver from 115
  the day the host *become* disunited.
The prophets will chant
  the " miserere " of the lost :
The druids will chant, 119
" Brython & sea co-eval will be."
The summer will not be sunshiny.
The barons will be overthrown — 122
  faint-heartedness will assail them.
  Beyond the border there had been spoil.
A thousand will test Prydein's line ; 125
  and him, who will greatly disturb the border
  I will not bewail : Let him avoid alders —
  alder copses befit the bottom of hell.
The adamantine firmament will be shaken
  by the Lord of the land everlasting. 130

ᛈ ᛈ ᛈ

Prophecies.

VERILY there will come a friendly ruler ; 1
  scarcely among men will they see his like.
In front of him will be widespread shouting.
  The army from bloodshed he will deliver. 4
If the trumpets of a warlike people be sounded
  he will cut down such as rush into the conflict.
Crows and chieftains delight in gore, 7
  and, on the scarlet path, unrestrained violence.
The leader will exalt his brave, brilliant host,
  and will face the army of the wild regions. 10

VERILY ruptures will come : A vow they
  will make at the very beginning of the year,
  which will profit the King along the coasts. 13

Gaeav, gyrr *wynt* llym—llywid longeu— 14
25 certh iawn ciliass*yn* mynud rhy·ffreu :
Pryd myr ryverthwy, ar warr tonneu,
77 *gwylein* ðy·gyrch dam o glawr brocheu.
Arth a llew ðer·llyv oleu bylleu : 18
2 Dibyn y tervyn ar ruð vereu.
Rhwy·geis*ir* cystuð—rhybuð rhag geu,
rhag y varanres *o* vawr greðeu. 21
Cwyðir tyrch torvoeð, dyrvynt daleu,
5 yng·hynniv gwaladr, o glod lathr gleu,
6 Dy·ðyrchavwyd torc*h* o barth Deheu, 24
y·gan was ry·ðadlas *am* i veu.

ÝN wir dy·ðyvi hael hy-ŵreð,
8 *a* dyrvawd volud mawr edrysseð.
llyw byrr, tew, lüyð, llydan i weð, 28
9 hyd ban vwynt seith *meib* i ri Gwyneð—
hyd ban dranghwy *llyw* dr*wy* *ff*awd ryveð.
11 Rhi eiðun ðy·hun '*n Reding* dudweð :
Treisant Eingl ar hynt o alltudeð : 32
12 Trwy vor yd lithrant a·u heisilleð.

ÝN wir dy·ðyvi teithïawg Von—
13 Drai*g* a diffreidiad o bobl Vrython :
Pen llüyð perchid lurigogion. 36
14 Dwvn y darogan dewin drywon
pebylliawnt a·r Dren a Tharanhon—
16 gor·lethant ðyvynt i geisaw Mon.
*H*off ðebed dy·hynt o Iwerðon : 40
17 Teg ffaw ði*ff*ygiaw Cesarogion.
Go·gan ang·harad o ðelwad heð :
19 Go·gan y perir cad arw yn neð— 43
Arth o Ðeheubarth gyvarth Wyneð
20 yn amwyn rhïyð,—rhyveð rosseð—
Yd heiðir all·tir a·i ðarmertheð— 46

184

Winter will send bitter winds that will control ships   14
  which would certainly withdraw at times of storm :
When the seas rush upon the crest of the waves
  gulls will snatch a morsel from the spume's surface.
Bear and lion will lap the shallow pools :   18
The boundary will depend on ruddy spears.
Hostages will be sought—a caution against treachery,
  against the marching army of mighty projects.   21
Standards of forces, which disturb the land, will be
  thrown down in fighting a leader of brilliant fame.
A standard was raised, on behalf of the South,   24
  by a youth who fought stoutly for his inheritance.

VERILY there will come a very brave prince,
  who will stir up eulogy *by* liberal largess.   27
A short, stout, broad-faced Ruler will wage war, until
  there will be seven sons to the prince of Gwyneδ—
  until *the Ruler* shall die by a strange fate.   30
The King will crave for his long rest *in Reading* soil :
  The Angles will pillage on their homeward journey :
  By sea, they and theirs will glide away.   33

VERILY there will come a true prince to Mon—
  a dragon and defender to the Brython people :
  The invading chief will respect his mailed warriors. 36
Confidently the diviner of the druids prophesies that
  they will pitch their tents on the Tern & Tarannon ;
  and will overwhelm those who will come to seize Mon.
Happy the departure of an expedition from Ireland : 40
  Fair the report of the failure of the King's warriors.
(The diviner) prophesies enmity in the guise of peace :
That a fierce war will be waged in the dingle :   43
That the Bear from the South will harass Gwyneδ,
  in defence of the King, a strange excess (of zeal) :
That the strange land and its crops will be attained : 46

185

77 Gaeav goleðir yn ℓeudireð — 47
　Rhy·lenwynt aesawr, yng·awr *o* gleð,
22　yng·hynniv gwaladr ar ior Gwyneð.

Ƿ N wir dy·ðaw awr dy·ðerbi hyn :
24 ℓLoegr*wys* ym·oℓyn oℓ vei genhyn. 51
　Gweler arðebed y gwyr brychwyn,
26　rha*g* saetheu, bereu, a haearn gwyn.
　Gelwhitor y·ar vor, a·u gwaewawr grŷn :
78 Nychawnt yn eigawn tra ℓüyðyn :
　Halltaw*g* ymyleð vyð eu bwðyn. 56

Ƿ N wir dy·ðyvi ði dra Havren
3　wrthredid Brydein, vrenhin gorðen.
ℓL*wrw* lywyð ℓïaws, ℓüyð i echen —
　Tëyrnas cy*n* adas ca*vas* v*l*aen. 60
5 Gwerin byd, yn wir, byðawnt lawen ;
　meðhawnt ar beiron, berthwyr echen.
7 lℓemychawd hireℓ ði uch Havren :
　Llwyth Kymry gynnuℓ yn ðiscowen 64
9　yng·hynniv gwaladr ; bythid lawen —
　pen rhi cerðorion, clod a weithen.

Ƿ N wir dy·ðaw cawr ; 67
10　a·i lu, a·i longawr ;
　a thorv yscwydawr ;
　a newyð waewawr. 70
12 A gwedy gwychr awr,
　i voð ev gwn*a*hawr.
　Cyrch*id ev Benvro* ; 73
13　fℓemychid yng·wo :
　Draig ni·d ym·gelho,
　er maint ð*el* iðo.
14 Nid yscawn ioled, 77
　orescyn Dyved.
15 Dy·ðyccawd niwed,
　tra merin Rheged. 80

186

That the winter will be spent in the cultivated parts :
That their swords will load their shields in war,
  in the attack of our leader on the lord of Gwyneδ. 49

VERILY the hour will come when we shall see
  the English collect all they have with them,
  and the departure of the fair, freckled men   52
  before arrows, spears, and flashing steel.
They will be challenged from the sea & their spearmen
  will shudder : they will perish in the water while
  marshalling : the salt sea-edges will be their tomb. 56

VERILY the King of destiny will come, from
  beyond Severn, and invade Prydein. This
  impetuous leader of the host will marshall his people—
  before he quitted *his* kingdom he received the crown.
Verily the populace will rejoice that the   61
  rich men of the nation will possess cauldrons.
A light will flash forth from upper Severn :
The Kymric race will assemble cheerfully   64
  in its leader's struggle, who will be merry—
  the chief patron of minstrels, the fanners of fame.

          VERILY a hero will come   67
            with his host and his ships :
            with a pile of shields,
            and brand new spears.   70
          And after a victorious shout,
            his will will be done.
          He will proceed *to Pembroke*,
            and blaze in his progress.   74
          A dragon may not hide himself,
            however many may oppose him.
          It is no slight praise,   77
            the vanquishing of Dyved.
          He will carry destruction,
            beyond the border of the March.   80

16 Peryv, perchen ced,   81
      wledych yn Elved.
    Hael, hydr y dy·liv ;
17   gor·vawr i gynniv.   84
    Wrth a wŷr i oðiv,
18 caffad gweith heiniv.   86

Darogan kad Waladr.

Marchawg *march* mwth, mysterin,
      a·r ðeu wyneb, beir vrwydrin—
80 Rhodiawg brad—ỻad i drenghi,
      ac yn Eryri i oloï.   4
20 Ban ðel cad waladr go·wna,
      yn·ôl, ym·Hrydein, ben ma ;
21 *a·i aml*wg oes moes nywia ;
      a·i ffinieu, vyð i·n vad·va.   8
22   Ys deubi, yna,
        Sais i erchi bwyta :
23 Dogn ŵyr : o *dra*
        rhyvyg, *t*roseða.   12
      Jeuhaw gwraig gan was
24   hên gas *a* nywia.
      Dogn ŵyr : o ryvyg
        tremyg—brad a wna.   16
25 A weleist vyng·har
        yn gware a·m pr*i*awd ?
      Gweleis gelein vain,
        a brain a·r ðygnawd.   20
26 Ac o·r rhy·ðamwein,
        gwaỻ grain cleðyvawd.
      Ac am lan . . . . . .

188

The lord, owner of tribute,　　81
will rule in Elved.
The prince boldly over-runs (the
country) very great his struggle. 84
With such as turn aside his stroke
a brisk encounter followed.　　86

Llewelyn and W. de Braose.

THE Knight of the swift, bay *horse*,　1
with the double face, creates turmoil:
With treachery afoot, a blessing his
death and burial in Snowdonia.　　4
When our war-lord comes he will make,
in a mead in Prydein, a chief place.
His manifest life will invigorate morals:
and his confines will be to us a an Eden.
There will come, thither,　　9
a Saxon seeking hospitality.
Grief he will know ; from excess
of presumption, he will sin.　　12
The yoking of a wife by a vassal
will renew old hatred : he will
know grief: from presumption
comes contempt ; he commits treason.　16
Did you see my friend
playing with my spouse?
I saw a slim corse,
and crows full of activity.　　20
But the catastrophe lacks the prostrate form of the sword-stroke.
And beyond the bank of　.　.　.

APPENDIX.*

Ⓜ AWR Ðuw ðigones   1
     heul hav, a·i ry·wres :
40·26 Ac Ev ðigones
     vuð coed, a mäes.   4
  23 Ys Ev a wehyð
     ðyliv nos a dyð :
  24 Dyð i·n annogaw ;
     nos i·n gor·ffwysaw.   8

     .   .   .   .

41.·18 Nu, nos cwð ðyvyð ?
  19 cw ðir·gêl rhag dyð ?
  20 Py ðug wyll gaeav ?
  21 Py gyrch ðechreu hâv ?   12
  19 A ŵyr ceïrð gelvyð
     py gêl calloryð ?
  20 Am·dyrr o·r anwe,
     o·r parth pan ðwyre.   16
42·3 Ev cyrch cerðorion
     seð Syberw Sëon.
41·21 Yn·ewis aethawg,
     ffysc ffo, ys ffodiawg.   20
  22 Ev di·hun hunawg ;
     Ev go·bryn Carawg—
  23 Cymry gaer-veðrawd,
     i dad Garadawg.   24
  24 Dïal Meneivron—
     dïal Mynawg Mon
     vawr, erch anudon.   27

*This Appendix contains several sections of poems
that seemed out of harmony with their surroundings.

APPENDIX.

THE great God ordained the   1
summer sun, & its great heat :
He also ordained the
  produce of wood and plain.   4
'T is He who weaves
  the warp of night and day :
The day for our activity ;
  the night for our rest.   8
        .   .   .   .
Now, the night, whence comes it ?
Where hides it from day ?
What took away winter's gloom ?
What fetches early summer ?   12
Knows the artificer of song
  what the cauldrons conceal ?
The song issues from the vapour —
  from that source it rises.   16
The artists resort to
  the seat of Seiont's Superbus.
In a painful dilemma,
  swift flight brings good luck.   20
He will rouse up the dead.
He will win Carog —
  Kymry's tumulus fort
  to the father of Caradog.   24
He will avenge Meneivron —
He, the prince of Mon, will avenge
  the great and terrible perjury.   27

The text of pages 190—198 should have appeared before the
Daroganeu, but was omitted by an oversight.

25 Gwenhwys vyℓt hirion   28
    ant Gaer Wyrangon.
42·1 Ev dy·vyδ Aeron
    y coel ganawon—
  2   y gor·weδw veibon.   32
    Ni·d an·chwarδ i alon
    roi i Ynyr wystlon.
  4   Neu·r di·ervis Rynn,
    ym·Horth Godoδin—   36
    y·moryd Uffin,
  5   esceirvrith vrenhin :
    i·w vraw, bor edewim.
  6   Wyv cerδenhin hen :   40
    Wyv cyvreu ℓawen—
  7   Athraw yn·Ygen :
    Meu, molawd Urien :
    Eirian i eiroes ;   44
  8   ℓyminawg, ℓwm *i* oes.
    Rhuδvedel, a anwys
    Ruδ-din, eℓyngwys.
    Caer—yr harδ Wenn wys—
    Ynyr a·i briwys.   49
11 Gweleis wyr gor·vawr
    a δy·gyrchynt awr :
12 Gweleis waed ar ℓawr   52
    rhac rhuthr cleδyvawr.
13 Glesynt escyℓ gwawr—
    Escorynt gwaewawr.   55
    Trychant golan
    cyman clodvawr—
    i vur a·i dir,
15   yn wir, cochawr.   59

192

The long-armed Gwentians   28
  will go to Worcester.
There will come to Aeron
  the petted whelps—
  the be-orphaned sons.   32
'T is no laughing matter to *John's*
  enemies to give him hostages.
He disarmed the promontory
  at the Gate of Godoðin ;   36
  and, at the great Ubban-ford,
  the shank-plaided King :
  To his fears I will leave the *Scot.*
I am an old wayfarer :   40
I am full of rejoicings :
I am a preceptor in Dygen :
Mine the praise of Owein :
Shining the purity of his life :   44
Austere and bare his living.
The gory reapers set free those
  whom Castell Coch contained.
The citadel, Gwenn's fair castle,   48
  King John destroyed it.
I saw the mighty men, who
  were rushing to the war-shout :
I saw blood on the ground spilt   52
  by the onslaught of the swordsmen.
As the wings of dawn grow grey
  the spearmen pour forth—
They cut down a fellow-soldier   56
  of outstanding eminence—
  His stronghold and land
  will, verily, be reddened.   59

Codiad yr Haul.

 ORRID mynudawl,   1
   duthiạwl, dân ysawl.
47 Ev iole*m*, uch llawr,
    dann tanllwythin gwawr—   4
21 uch awel—uchel !
    Uch no phob nyvel,
    mawr i a·nyvel.
22 Ni thrig yng·o·vyr,   8
    noc yn·heithawr llyr :
23 *Dy*·lwybr yr ebyr—
    dyval yng·hynvyr.
24 Gwawr wenn wrth uchyr ;   12
    gwen wrth wâr, wrth wrŷs—
    wrth bob hevelis—
25 wrth *bilis* Nwython—
    wrth bevr Avaon.   16
26 Arδwyreav a varn
    wryseδ y cadarn.
48 Trydar *galanas*—
    hir *a* dwvn i gas.   20
 . Ni·d mi gwr llwvr llwyd
    δy·grwydr wrth *hel* bwyd.
2 Hud vyng·hleu garant—
    cleu, di·var, di·chwant.   24
3 *Ac* o·m llaw i·th law
    ni δyd dwy*ll* δim *maw*.

 4 Tri·thri march noded—
    y cor a·r enwed—   28
    A·r *naw*, meirch meiawg,
5 oeδynt go·wythawg :
    Oeδ march Caradawg
    gyvrwy teithïawg :   32

Sunrise.

PUNCTUAL the orb of   1
 consuming fire bursts forth.
We should give thanks for the spread
 of the blaze of dawn above the   4
 earth—above the breeze, high !
Above every cloud,
 great the brilliance !
The *sun* abides not in the bays,   8
 nor in the reaches of the tides.
It traverses the estuaries, &
 is unceasing on the high seas.
Pearly dawn repels the powers of   12
 darkness : it smiles upon everything alike, both tame and wild :
 upon the *skin-clad* Nwython—
 upon the spruce Avaon.   16
I extol Him, who condemns
 the violence of the strong.
The din *of carnage*—
 long and deep the horror of it.   20
I am not a shy, pale fellow,
 who wanders as he begs his fare.
Enchantment is my trusty friend—
 faithful, spleenless, without greed.   24
And from me to you counterfeit will
 pass on nothing tangible.

Thrice three horses were noted—
 the team was named—   28
 and the *nine* war-steeds
 were somewhat mettlesome.
The steed of Caradawg
 was a perfect saddle-horse :   32

48 6 *Velly* march Gwythur ;   33
Ⅰ *Hevyd* march Gwarδur.
 7 *Pedweryδ vu i* Arthur—
     ehovn rhoδ*ei* gur.   36
 8 A march Taliessin ;
     A phevr, Ⅱedvegin
 9 varch ⅠLeu, ⅠLwydin :
     A Grei varch Cunin.   40
10 *Wythved,* Awyδawg,
     march cynhei*l* voδawg.
     Du—mor oeδ enwawg—
11 march Brwyn, vron vradawg. 44

   A·r tri charnavlawg—
12 ni·d ant hynt halawg :
     Kethin varch Keidaw—
13 carn *g*avr oeδ arnaw.   48
     Yscwyδ-vrith, Goδig,
14 gorwyδ ⅠLemenig.
     March Rhyδerch—Rhyδig
15 Ⅱwyd, Ⅱiw eⅡeïg,
     Ⅱamei·n Ⅱawn elwig.   52
16 ⅠFroenvoⅡ, gwyrenhig
     oeδ march Sadyrnin,
     a march Custenhin ;   56
17 Ac ereiⅡ yn trin,
     rhag tir aⅡwe*r*in.

18 Henwyn mad δy·δug,
     chweδl o Hiraδug,   60

19 Bum hwch, a bum bwch ;
     Bum syw, a bum swch :
     Bum banw ; bum banhwch :
20 Bum gawr ym·rythwch :   64

So, the horse of Gwythur ;   33
  and, also, that of Gwarδur.
The Fourth was Arthur's,
  who fearlessly inflicted pain.   36
And the horse of Taliesin ;
And ᴌwydin, the fine,
  half-trained horse of ᴌeu.
Also Grei the horse of Cunin.   40
The eighth, Awyδawg was
  a pleasing horse to carry one.
And Ebony, that was so famous,
  the steed of traitorous Brwyn.   44

There are three cloven-footed : these
  will not go on a knavish expedition :—
Kethin, the steed of Keidaw,
  had the hooves of a goat :   48
Goδig, the steed of ᴌemenig,
  was pied-shouldered :
Rhyδig, the steed of Rhyδerch —
  a pear-coloured grey,   52
  would leap full of spirit.
Wide-nostrilled, and active
  was the horse of Sadyrnin,
  and the horse of Custenhin,   56
  as well as others in battle
  against the land of the strangers.
Henwyn, the gentle, brought
  the story from Hiraδug.   60

I was a sow ; I was a buck :
I was a wizard ; I was a share :
I was a store pig ; I was a store sow :
I was a hero in trouble :   64

Bum *or*·lliv yn eirth :
21 Bum ton yn eng·eirth :   67
Bum cavn *yn·istryw*
. ysceinad Dilyw.
22 Bum caeth ar dri phren :
Bum pell, *a* bum pen.
Bum gynran gwala,   71
welei olwg dra.
24 Gres mire morva,
cadwent geneδl δa.

25 O·r vyδ is awyr,   75
gwedy caffer gwir,
26 Ni·d byw *neb yn llwyr*
wr*th* voδ maint a·i gŵyr. 78

I was a great current on the slopes :
I was a wave in the plains :
I was a (ferry)-boat in the destruc-
tive spread of the flood :   68
I was a captive on the cross :
I went afar, and I was chief :
I was a leader, with abundance,
who saw beyond the present.   72
Welcome the aspect of the salt marsh,
which protected the good people.

Of those that be beneaththe sky, 75
when all the truth is bare,
none lives entirely to the mind
of such as know him there.   78

198

POSTSCRIPT.

BESIDES the poems given on pages 2-198 there are certain other poems of a theological nature. These appear to belong to the second or third quarter of the xiiith century, and cannot, therefore, be the work of Taliesin. However, they have been edited and translated, and will, I trust, appear in a supplementary booklet, or find a hospitable corner in some publication. The following is a list of the omitted matter.

Marwnat y vil veib ..	..	..	3-7
Dews Duw delwat ..	..	..	10-12
Iloer yn anlles, l. 20	..	..	37-38
Plaeu yr Eifft	..	..	44-45
Ilath Moesen ..	..	..	46-47
Ar clawr elvyδ	..	..	52
Ryveδav nachiawr	..	..	52
Ad Duw meiδat	..	..	53-54
Trindawd tragywyδ ..	..	..	73-74
Gwawr Iluyδ mawr	..	..	74-76
Ymarwar Iluyδ bychan	..	..	78
Kanu y byt mawr ..	..	..	79-80

FINIS.